Encounters with Jesus

Meet the Lord

James J. DiGiacomo, S.J.
John Walsh, M.M.

Winston Press

Acknowledgements

Scripture texts used in this work (except for Luke 24:35 and Acts 2:42) are taken from the *Good News Bible,* copyright © 1976, by the American Bible Society. All rights reserved.

Luke 24:35 and Acts 2:42 are from *The Jerusalem Bible,* copyright © 1966 by Darton, Longman and Todd Ltd. and Doubleday and Company, Inc.

© 1977 by Winston Press, Inc.
Library of Congress Catalog Card Number: 77-72548
ISBN: 0-03-021281-2
Printed in the United States of America

Nihil Obstat: David A. Dillon
Imprimatur: + John A. Roach
Archbishop of St. Paul and Minneapolis
March 22, 1977

Photo Credits:
Gene Ahrens *8*
John Arms *17, 78*
Camerique *86*
Berne Greene *56*
Freda Leinwand *opposite 1*
Joan Mitchell *72*
Cyril A. Reilly *25, 32, 36, 62, 66, 81*
Casey Streich *92*
Strix Pix *51*

Contents

INTRODUCTION

"Show us the Father"

"Show us the Father!"

Twelve men sat around a supper table. One was a leader; the others were his loyal followers. None but the leader suspected that he had less than twenty-four hours to live, and that he had just eaten his Last Supper with them.

He was their leader because they were convinced that he was God's spokesman, sent to reveal to them their Father who was in heaven. Being with him, watching him, and listening to him, they felt close to God in a very special way. Tonight they were troubled and sad, because he had just told them that he must leave them and return to his Father.

> Philip said to him, "Lord, show us the Father; that is all we need."
>
> Jesus answered, "For a long time I have been with you all; yet you do not know me, Philip? Whoever has seen me has seen the Father. Why, then, do you say, 'Show us the father'?"—*John 14:8-9*

Christians believe that the way to God is through Jesus Christ. For them, he is the best means to find themselves, to relate to other people through love, and to achieve union with God. They come in contact with God through Jesus in many ways, but one special way is through the New Testament of the Bible. The gospel accounts of the life, death, and resurrection of Christ can put a person in touch with him, for a Christian reverences these accounts as the Word of God addressed to each of us personally here and now.

This book was written to help you read the gospels and come in living contact with Jesus Christ, that he may reveal the Father to you and share his life with you. Many people need help to read the gospels, for the people who told the Jesus story lived in a time and place far removed from us, with a mentality and a style that create problems even for well-educated, intelligent people.

To put it most simply: this book is offered as an Encounter Causer. What you need is not just information about God or facts about Jesus. These have their place, but they aren't the heart of the matter. To really know someone and to relate to him or her as a friend, you need to encounter people, to *meet* them on an interpersonal level. What we want, after all, is not to be experts on God, but to *know* God. Becoming a Scripture scholar is nice, but becoming a Christian is better. Being a theologian has its advantages, but it's far more important to be a person of faith, in touch with God and sharing his life.

Can this book do all that? Yes, it can. Not all by itself, of course, and not by any kind of magic. You see, we are convinced that God thinks and cares about you even when he's the farthest thing from your mind. If you open yourself to him and give his Son a chance to reach you, we have no doubt that it can and will happen.

How does it work? Well, let's stop talking and start doing. We can start the way two young friends of Jesus started, by being introduced to him. It was on the banks of the Jordan river, where a charismatic figure named John the Baptist was leading a religious revival. Come back in imagination to that far-off day, and

Meet the Lord.

First Friends

The next day John was standing there again with two of his disciples, when he saw Jesus walking by. "There is the Lamb of God!" he said.

The two disciples heard him say this and went with Jesus. Jesus turned, saw them following him, and asked, "What are you looking for?"

They answered, "Where do you live, Rabbi?" (This word means "Teacher.")

"Come and see," he answered. (It was then about four o'clock in the afternoon.) So they went with him and saw where he lived, and spent the rest of that day with him.

One of them was Andrew, Simon Peter's brother. At once he found his brother Simon and told him, "We have found the Messiah." (This word means "Christ.") Then he took Simon to Jesus.

Jesus looked at him and said, "Your name is Simon son of John, but you will be called Cephas." (This is the same as Peter and means "a rock.")

The next day Jesus decided to go to Galilee. He found Philip and said to him, "Come with me!" (Philip was from Bethsaida, the town where Andrew and Peter lived.) Philip found Nathanael and told him, "We have found the one whom Moses wrote about in the book of the Law and whom the prophets also wrote about. He is Jesus son of Joseph, from Nazareth."—*John 1:35-45*

"Where do you Live?"

They were two young fishermen, caught up in the religious revival that centered around John the Baptist. They had no idea, the morning of that fateful day, that before the sun set the whole direction of their lives would be changed. Even at the day's end, they still didn't realize what had happened to them. There was nothing dramatic or spectacular about their encounter with the young carpenter from Nazareth. It all happened so quietly, so unobtrusively —a chance meeting, an invitation to spend a few hours, a conversation that started tentatively and grew more earnest, and a promise to come again and bring some friends. John never dreamed that many, many years later, when he was a very old man, he would recall so clearly that they met at four o'clock in the afternoon.

He and Andrew always looked back on that evening as the turning point in their lives. Behind them was the world of other young men on fishing boats, looking forward to getting out on their own, marrying and raising a family, finding their place in the small, busy town on the lake shore in Galilee. It was a safe, predictable, conventional world with few surprises. Ahead of them was an unbelievable series of events—the restless journeys crisscrossing Palestine, the unforgettable sermons, the signs and wonders, the shifting moods of the crowds, the violent end on the hill of crucifixion, and the explosion of new life with the risen Lord. And then their own ministry, the beginnings of the Church, and the scattering abroad to conquer new worlds.

What a turnaround! And it all began with a brief encounter and a few hours together. What did they talk about that first day? What could have started such incredible events in motion?

Most likely it was a very ordinary conversation. It wasn't *what* they talked about, but the effect they had on one another. John and Andrew were idealistic young men, looking for something bigger than the small world that beckoned to them. That's what attracted them to the Baptist and brought them to the banks of the Jordan in the days of their youth. So when the prophet pointed out Jesus to them, they followed—timidly at first, and at a distance. That was when the stranger turned around.

"What are you looking for?"

What are we looking for? How can we answer that one, when we don't know ourselves? How can we put into words the emptiness, the longing for something bigger that we've ever known, something better than we've ever looked forward to? We'd feel foolish if we tried to express in words the desires that we can hardly name ourselves.

"Where do you live?"

"Come and see."

And that's how it all began. An attitude of openness on their part, a simple invitation accepted, a little time spent together. They didn't know it yet, but from that moment on, nothing would ever be the same again.

The remarkable thing about this story is that it still happens. Every day people meet Jesus Christ and, by their own admission, are changed. They're convinced that in meeting Christ they're coming in touch with the living God who transforms them by his grace and opens up horizons they never dreamed of. They're poor people and rich people, struggling people and successful people, scholars and illiterates and in-between. They're men and women, old and young, of every race and nationality, and they all agree on one thing: it can happen to you, too. All you need is to be open, to accept an invitation, to spend a little time together . . . and be willing to go wherever he leads. Pry open the lid on your heart, expand your desires, and make yourself available for a new world of experience. Start with the simple question "Where do you live?" and be willing to come and see.

This book is a story and an invitation. We're going to tell, once again, the story of Jesus and the people in his life. And we're inviting you to share it—not as a spectator watching other people from another time and place, but as one of the characters in a real-life drama that's unfolding right now, which you and God can write together.

We're not simply going to re-tell the story the way you have heard it many times before. Rather, we will dwell on several incidents in the Gospel narrative when Jesus encounters other people, to see how they affect one another, and what happens to them. And we'll try to see if we're in the story, too.

This book is addressed to you in the conviction that God became man in Jesus Christ in order to encounter you and me and to establish love relationships between us. We believe that a prayerful study of Jesus' encounters with people can help us meet God in him and in one another. We're convinced that his Word has this power, that his grace is available to us if we but open ourselves to him. If you have trouble relating to a far-off, distant, faceless God, then join us and draw near to him who first loved us. He has a question for you: What are you looking for? And if you want to know where he lives, come and see.

If you're not too rushed, and are willing to spend a few hours with the Son of God, you can meet him in a very personal way. He won't force himself on you, but if you take the risk that goes with any human encounter, there's no telling where it may lead. For John and Andrew it was a small beginning that led to greatness.

Things to do
1. Who encouraged Andrew and John to seek out Jesus?
2. When John and Andrew decided to follow Jesus instead of pursuing their careers as fishermen, do you think their parents and neighbors all approved? Do you see young people acting this way today?
3. In your opinion, what was it about Jesus that attracted these young men and drew them to him?
4. How was this first encounter with Jesus a turning point in their lives?
5. This incident, and the succeeding ones in this book, took place over 1900 years ago. How can they be about us?
6. What are *you* looking for?

Signs and Wonders

Signs and Wonders

That first encounter between Jesus and his friends was the beginning of his public ministry. The next couple of years were filled with other meetings, with signs and wonders. He taught the people, healed their sicknesses of body and soul, and gained an enthusiastic following. He also gained enemies, as the leaders of the religious establishment came to regard him as a threat to their position. As it turned out, his enemies were more determined and better organized than his friends. But more of that later.

His ministry was mostly in Galilee, in the north of Palestine, and occasionally in Jerusalem, the political and religious capital of the nation. During those years he met all kinds of people who reacted to him and his message in an extraordinary variety of ways. Gradually it became clear what was happening: people were choosing up sides, either for him or against him. The stakes were high, and the game was for keeps.

This whole book is about the people whose paths crossed that of Jesus of Nazareth and whose lives were decisively affected by that meeting. In this first part we'll look closely at five meetings:

—An unplanned fishing trip;

—A secret night meeting with a religious leader;

—A meeting with a tax collector up a tree;

—A crowd with a craving for food but not for faith;

—A woman who came looking for water and found herself.

As you watch these people meet Christ, you may also encounter him in a new way. And don't be surprised if you meet yourself, too.

A Marvelous Catch of Fish

One day Jesus was standing on the shore of Lake Gennesaret while the people pushed their way up to him to listen to the word of God. He saw two boats pulled up on the beach; the fishermen had left them and were washing the nets. Jesus got into one of the boats—it belonged to Simon—and asked him to push off a little from the shore. Jesus sat in the boat and taught the crowd.

When he finished speaking, he said to Simon, "Push the boat out further to the deep water, and you and your partners let down your nets for a catch."

"Master," Simon answered, "we worked hard all night long and caught nothing. But if you say so, I will let down the nets." They let them down and caught such a large number of fish that the nets were about to break. So they motioned to their partners in the other boat to come and help them. They came and filled both boats so full of fish that the boats were about to sink. When Simon Peter saw what had happened, he fell on his knees before Jesus and said, "Go away from me, Lord! I am a sinful man!"

He and the others with him were all amazed at the large number of fish they had caught. The same was true of Simon's partners, James and John, the sons of Zebedee. Jesus said to Simon, "Don't be afraid; from now on you will be catching men."

They pulled the boats up on the beach, left everything, and followed Jesus—*Luke 5:1-11*

"From now on you will be catching men"

There's nothing unusual about finding a beach too crowded, but this was different. Everyone was pushing and shoving for the best places to hear a charismatic young preacher. It was a rock-concert promoter's dream—a sellout, with even standing room hard to find. That was how Jesus, early in his public life, affected people. Without promotion, without gimmicks, simply through the quiet power of his fascinating personality, he drew them. And he held them with nothing but words.

The words were deceptively simple. He told stories drawn from the everyday world of farmers, shopkeepers, and housewives. In language that the least educated could understand, he told them about their lives, about God their father, about the care and the plans he had for them.

As they listened, they felt better about themselves and closer to God. That's why they were here on the lake shore today, instead of cleaning the house or minding the store. They didn't want to miss a word.

Jesus didn't want to disappoint them, so he had a good idea. Simon Peter, one of the young fishermen who was between trips, had beached his boat. He used to spend much of his spare time with a small group who had attached themselves informally to Jesus. So he was somewhat flattered, and eager to help, when the young preacher asked to use his boat for a pulpit. This was pretty smart, for now the people couldn't crowd around too close without getting their feet wet, and Jesus had a good spot from which to address them.

Peter felt good when the talk was over; he was glad he had been able to help. For a while, listening to Jesus, he had forgotten the disappointment of the previous night's fishing trip. It had been a wipeout. Hours of back-breaking work, rowing and casting and hauling, and nothing to show for it. Well, he thought, you win a few and lose a few; maybe tonight the fish will cooperate. Meanwhile it's good to rest and listen to my new friend.

So he was quite taken aback when Jesus made his unexpected suggestion: "While we're out here in the water, let's drop the nets and catch some fish." How do you like that?! He's a good carpenter and a great preacher, but he doesn't know anything about fishing. It's the wrong time and the wrong place; we found that out last night.

Better to wait for dark and try a different location. And the men are tired. Why not quit while we're behind?

All these thoughts came to Peter's mind, and they were almost on his lips, when something made him pause. There was something about the way Jesus made the request, something in his manner that made him reconsider. He knows what I'm thinking, but he wants me to trust him. The practical, down-to-earth realist in me says "Forget it!" The other side of me—the dreamer, the adventurer—says "Why not? You never can tell what may happen!"

So Simon Peter trusted Jesus and took a chance. He and his men rowed into deep water and let down the nets. Have you ever seen the fishing nets used on the Sea of Galilee? They're big and clumsy, and a sweep with them takes a lot of hard work. The men were tired from a fruitless night's fishing, and they had no realistic hope of scoring this time. But Jesus was a hard man to say no to, and some instinct stronger than prudence led them on.

What a shock when the school of fish struck the nets! For a while, as they dragged the catch into the boat and frantically signalled the men in the other boat to help, they were too busy even to be amazed. But when it was all over, and they had beached the boats and unloaded their tremendous catch, a profound sense of awe took hold of them. Now it dawned on them that they were in the presence of some mysterious power beyond their experience or comprehension. Peter was the first to put this feeling into words: "Go away from me, Lord! I am a sinful man!" In the presence of the holy and the sacred, he was painfully aware of his faults. Maybe if he were perfect he'd feel at home with Jesus; as it was, the gulf between them was too much to bear.

This is the way people often feel about God. They'd rather wait until they're perfect before they try to get close to him. Overwhelmed by their own shortcomings, they can't imagine God wanting to have anything to do with them.

To Peter, and to every person who has ever felt this way, Jesus has a simple, reassuring answer: "Don't be afraid." And then the clincher! "From now on you will be catching men." This spectacular catch of fish is just a sign pointing to something much greater. Some day soon they'll win the minds and hearts of men and women and bring them to Christ. That will be the real miracle—not a net bulging with fish, but the triumph of God's grace in people's hearts, through the ministry of imperfect, sinful human beings.

At that moment, Peter and John and Andrew and the others

knew what they'd been looking for, and that they'd found it. "They left everything, and followed Jesus."

Jesus worked a miracle that day because Peter let him. Peter trusted Jesus and took a chance. If he hadn't opened himself up to the new experiences available in that encounter, nothing would have happened. All sorts of possibilities in him would never have been realized. And history would long since have forgotten—indeed, never known—about a few Galilean fishermen in an obscure town. An invitation from Christ, and the acceptance of that invitation in the spirit of trust and adventure, made all the difference.

Could the same thing happen to you? Well, why do you suppose he did it? For the fish?

Things to do
1. Why did Jesus ask Simon for the use of his boat?
2. Why were the fishermen reluctant to cast their nets?
3. Why did Peter ask Jesus to leave him?
4. We are told that after this sign they "became his followers." But they had been in his company some time before this. Explain.
5. Did you ever take a wild chance against your better judgment, the way they did when they let down the nets? What happened?
6. Do you know of any person in history or in fiction—books, movies, TV—who had an experience like this?
7. If Peter and the others had been prudent and sensible and left the nets out to dry, how would that have changed their lives?

Nicodemus

There was a Jewish leader named Nicodemus, who belonged to the party of the Pharisees.

One night he went to Jesus and said to him, "Rabbi, we know that you are a teacher sent by God. No one could perform the miracles you are doing unless God were with him."

Jesus answered, "I am telling you the truth: no one can see the Kingdom of God unless he is born again."

"How can a grown man be born again?" Nicodemus asked. "He certainly cannot enter his mother's womb and be born a second time!"

"I am telling you the truth," replied Jesus, "that no one can enter the Kingdom of God unless he is born of water and the Spirit. A person is born physically of human parents, but he is born spiritually of the Spirit. Do not be surprised because I tell you that you must all be born again. The wind blows wherever it wishes; you hear the sound it makes, but you do not know where it comes from or where it is going. It is like that with everyone who is born of the Spirit."

For God loved the world so much that he gave his only Son, so that everyone who believes in him may not die but have eternal life.
—*John 3:1-8,16*

You must be born again

One of the striking things about Jesus and the way he related to people was his ability to adapt to them. With farmers and fishermen and merchants he spoke in simple, picturesque terms, using stories and examples taken from their workaday world. With learned religious leaders like Nicodemus he could speak the subtle language of rabbinical theology. He met people where they were, but he didn't leave them there. While accepting them for the persons they were, he challenged them to go further—to broaden their horizons and break out of the narrow, comfortable world in which they might become stagnant.

Nicodemus was trying to play both sides of the street. As a member of the Sanhedrin, he associated with men who were bitter enemies of Christ. Yet he had been deeply impressed by the young prophet, and wanted to be his disciple. The only way he could do this, without surrendering his influential position on the Council, was to visit Jesus secretly at night. Jesus accepted him on these terms; he didn't insist on a decision, at least not just now. Indeed, he made himself available and helped Nicodemus find his own way in his own good time.

But he doesn't let Nicodemus stand still, either. He shakes him up with the mysterious assertion that if he wishes to be a success, he must be born again. Nicodemus doesn't know what Jesus means, so he pretends to take him literally: "How can a grown man be born again?" But Jesus pushes on. Instead of explaining, he gets in deeper. A man must be born again of water and the Spirit. Jesus here is challenging Nicodemus to go beyond the clever games of the learned and plunge into mysteries too deep to be understood. He is saying, in effect, "Nicodemus, I don't care how smart you are. There are things both in nature and in the world of the spirit that you will never fully understand. Just because you don't fully understand them, it doesn't mean that they're any less real."

Many people think that mysteries are something found only in religion. But they're all around us. For example, take the wind. As Jesus points out to Nicodemus, we can't see the wind (though we can hear it). We don't know where it comes from or where it goes. But even though we don't understand it, we still believe in it. If we didn't, many things would get blown away—even, sometimes, ourselves. We

don't understand electricity either, or a thousand things revealed to us under the scientist's microscope. And we don't fully understand people, who are perhaps the most mysterious of all, because they're like God.

In speaking to Nicodemus, Jesus is addressing those educated, cultured people who like their universe served up logical and intellectually respectable. These are the sophisticates who are embarrassed and uncomfortable with mystery because it looks too much like superstition. He tells them (us?) that the search for God calls for much more than brains. It calls for trust, for a willingness to accept truths our minds can't comprehend.

Does this present a problem? Of course it does. An intelligent person tries to develop a critical mind. This is wise, because every day all kinds of people try to make us believe all kinds of nonsense . . . and not just in television commercials, either. But the kind of faith we're talking about, and the faith that Jesus wants, isn't the same as being gullible. He doesn't so much ask us to believe *things* as to believe *him*. When Nicodemus said, "We know you are a teacher sent from God," that was a statement of faith. It meant he was ready to be led further, to go deeper into the mystery of life in God. So Jesus lets him in on the great secret he had come to reveal: that we're all meant to be born again in Baptism, that a new and wonderful life is there waiting for us, if we choose to accept it.

Once we believe in Jesus Christ, a whole new world can open up for us. Like Nicodemus, we'll be asked to believe things, just on his word, that sound almost too good to be true. Such as: "For God loved the world so much that he gave his only Son, so that everyone who believes in him may not die but have eternal life."

Things to do
1. Why did Nicodemus visit Jesus at night?
2. Who were the Sanhedrin?
3. How do Christians interpret Jesus' statement that a person must be born again?
4. Is it more difficult for intelligent and educated people to be religious? Explain.
5. "Christians believe not in some*thing* but in some*one*." Explain.

Zacchaeus

Jesus went on into Jericho and was passing through. There was a chief tax collector there named Zacchaeus, who was rich. He was trying to see who Jesus was, but he was a little man and could not see Jesus because of the crowd. So he ran ahead of the crowd and climbed a sycamore tree to see Jesus, who was going to pass that way. When Jesus came to that place, he looked up and said to Zacchaeus, "Hurry down, Zacchaeus, because I must stay in your house today."

Zacchaeus hurried down and welcomed him with great joy. All the people who saw it started grumbling, "This man has gone as a guest to the home of a sinner!"

Zacchaeus stood up and said to the Lord, "Listen, sir! I will give half my belongings to the poor, and if I have cheated anyone, I will pay him back four times as much."

Jesus said to him, "Salvation has come to this house today, for this man, also, is a descendant of Abraham. The Son of Man came to seek and to save the lost." —*Luke 19:1-10*

Out on a Limb

Sometimes we imagine that traveling with Jesus was like moving around in a portable church. You know—very solemn. Like everybody standing around praying or looking up to heaven or at least very serious. Jesus making profound statements, and the apostles checking their notes to make sure they got it down right. ("Did you get that one about turning the other cheek?")

Of course it wasn't that way at all. Sometimes people did really wild things, like taking a roof apart to let a sick man down where Jesus could cure him. Then there was the tax collector who climbed the tree. His name was Zacchaeus. In Jericho he was nobody's favorite person. Zacchaeus was a bad guy because he made his living collecting taxes for the Romans. Anybody who worked for the hated Romans was looked down on, but a tax collector was the lowest form of life. He was not your basic IRS person, who's not high on the Top Forty but does what most people consider an honest, respectable job. The tax-gathering system in the Roman empire was shot through with corruption from top to bottom. Even if the Romans had not been hated as pagan occupying forces, their tax collectors would have been despised, and usually on merit.

So the day that Jesus passed through Jericho, Zacchaeus had a problem. As usual, there was a big crowd, and the pushing and shoving made it hard to get a good spot where you could see him. It was doubly difficult for a man like Zacchaeus who was a) unpopular and b) short. Other little guys could get to the front because people could see over them, but nobody was going to let that rotten little grafter through. So what could he do? So climb a tree.

It wasn't the most dignified thing he could have done. Nobody looks twice when a kid climbs a tree. But the local IRS man? Well, this was no ordinary day for Zacchaeus. Something about the arrival of the young preacher from Galilee had him all steamed up. What was it that made him climb that tree? Was it just curiosity? Or was there a feeling of urgency that he could sense but not define? From what happened later, we can guess that Zacchaeus wasn't happy with his life so far, that he was looking for something he couldn't name. Maybe he had a secret ambition to be an honest man. Maybe he just wanted to stop being a social outcast and have some friends besides other tax collectors. Whatever it was, the appearance of Jesus brought it to a head. He just had to get a look at him. If you asked him why, he couldn't have told you.

Well, you know what happened. He not only got to see Jesus, he met him and talked with him. First there was that unforgettable moment when Jesus looked up into the branches of the sycamore tree and saw him. There have been some silly debates over the years about whether Jesus ever laughed. If he didn't laugh at that moment, he certainly must have cracked a great big smile. Nobody else was smiling; seeing Zacchaeus was enough to spoil anybody's day.

Then Jesus made one of those totally unexpected gestures that were his trademark. He didn't just greet Zacchaeus and draw attention to him. He invited himself to dinner! You must understand that in that social situation, it was the greatest honor that Jesus could have done him. And it was accepted as such. It delighted Zacchaeus and infuriated his enemies. If there was one sure way to lose popularity with the respectable townspeople, this was it.

But there was more to Jesus' behavior than met the eye. He wasn't just making a flamboyant, unconventional gesture to shake up the placid burghers of Jericho. In a most improbable way, he was encountering Zacchaeus. This was no mere social meeting. There was a chemistry between the two men that was volatile and potentially explosive. For Jesus sensed why Zacchaeus had climbed that tree and what he was really looking for. For a moment, there was no jostling crowd, no eager disciples, no hostile bystanders. There were only the two of them, and for one it was the turning point in his life.

Up till now, Jesus had all the good lines in the drama. He had taken the initiative, met Zacchaeus more than halfway, and responded generously to the other's timid overture. Now it was Zacchaeus' turn. He saw the resentment in his neighbors' eyes, heard their muttered complaints. How could he show them—and himself —that Jesus hadn't made a mistake? The answer was simple, but he was as amazed as they were to hear it from his own lips: ". . . if I have cheated anyone, I will pay him back four times as much." (Wow! Did I say that?)

He said it, all right, and he must have meant it, for Jesus said that salvation came to Zacchaeus' house that day. There are a few things worth noting here. First, he must have done more than his share of cheating; otherwise his pledge to make restitution would have made no sense. Secondly, he must have been feeling guilty long before he ever climbed that tree; his conversion could hardly have happened so instantaneously. Finally, he had a lot of changes to make in his style of living and his relationship with others. It wouldn't be easy to go to the people who hated him and return their money.

Yes, Zacchaeus might have trouble adjusting to his new way of life. On the other hand, he could now live with himself. He felt like a new man. He'd show his neighbors that his conversion was no mere flash in the pan. He still had to prove himself, but he felt that now he could. He'd said it in front of Jesus, so there was no turning back.

You might say that Zacchaeus went out on a limb that day. He came down that tree a changed man. Jesus affected people that way. He perceives possibilities in us that no one else—not even ourselves —can. He makes the first move to encounter us, and if we're brave enough to respond we can be changed for the better. It's scary, but if we can believe in ourselves half as much as he does, it's easy. Almost as easy as falling out of a tree.

Things to do

1. Why did Zacchaeus have to climb a tree to see Jesus?
2. How did the townspeople feel about Jesus going to Zacchaeus' house for dinner? Why?
3. Zacchaeus made a big change in his life that day. What do you think turned him around?
4. Zacchaeus said that if he had cheated anyone he would pay back four times as much. Wasn't he overdoing it? Do you think he meant it? Did he keep his promise?
5. If Zacchaeus were your father, how would you feel about his decision? Why? What would you tell him?
6. Do you think Zacchaeus really changed that much? What is he going to have to do to make his resolution stick? Can he do it?

Multiplication of the Loaves

After this, Jesus went across Lake Galilee (or, Lake Tiberias, as it is also called). A large crowd followed him, because they had seen his miracles of healing the sick. Jesus went up a hill and sat down with his disciples. The time for the Passover Festival was near. Jesus looked around and saw that a large crowd was coming to him, so he asked Philip, "Where can we buy enough food to feed all these people?" (He said this to test Philip; actually he already knew what he would do.)

Philip answered, "For everyone to have even a little, it would take more than two hundred silver coins to buy enough bread."

Another one of his disciples, Andrew, who was Simon Peter's brother, said, "There is a boy here who has five loaves of barley bread and two fish. But that will certainly not be enough for all these people."

"Make the people sit down," Jesus told them. (There was a lot of grass there.) So all the people sat down; there were about five thousand men. Jesus took the bread, gave thanks to God, and distributed it to the people who were sitting there. He did the same with the fish, and they all had as much as they wanted. When they were all full, he said to his disciples, "Gather the pieces left over; let us not waste a bit." So they gathered them all and filled twelve baskets with the pieces left over from the five barley loaves which the people had eaten.

Next Day
When the people found Jesus on the other side of the lake, they said to him, "Teacher, when did you get here?"

Jesus answered, "I am telling you the truth: you are looking for me because you ate the bread and had all you wanted, not because you understood my miracles. Do not work for food that spoils; instead, work for the food that lasts for eternal life. This is the food which the Son of Man will give you, because God, the Father, has put his mark of approval on him.

"For the bread that God gives is he who comes down from heaven and gives life to the world."

"Sir," they asked him, "give us this bread always."

"I am the bread of life," Jesus told them. "He who comes to me will never be hungry; he who believes in me will never be thirsty."

"I am the living bread that came down from heaven. If anyone eats this bread, he will live forever. The bread that I will give him is my flesh, which I give so that the world may live."

This started an angry argument among them. "How can this man give us his flesh to eat?" they asked.

Jesus said to them, "I am telling you the truth: if you do not eat the flesh of the Son of Man and drink his blood, you will not have life in yourselves. Whoever eats my flesh and drinks my blood has eternal life, and I will raise him to life on the last day. For my flesh is the real food; my blood is the real drink. Whoever eats my flesh and drinks my blood lives in me, and I live in him."

Many of his followers heard this and said, "This teaching is too hard. Who can listen to it?"

Because of this, many of Jesus' followers turned back and would not go with him any more. So he asked the twelve disciples, "And you—would you also like to leave?"

Simon Peter answered him, "Lord, to whom would we go? You have the words that give eternal life. And now we believe and know that you are the Holy One who has come from God." —*John 6:1-13, 25-27, 33-35, 51-56, 60, 66-69*

The Bread of Life

When people visit the lake shore area where Jesus fed the crowd with the loaves and fish, the question hits them right away: What was the problem? They weren't very far from nearby towns. If he had sent them away to find a late supper for themselves, it would have been an inconvenience—nothing more. The miracle was unnecessary; was it performed, then, just for show? No, certainly not that; Jesus never used his power merely to astound or impress, but only to serve people's needs. Why, then, did they need this miracle? Not because they needed bread, but because they needed a sign.

When we love someone very much, we want to give that person not just presents or words or even deeds. We want to give ourselves. In this we are like God, who was not content to send prophets or to save his people from afar. He had to go all the way and become one of us, in Jesus Christ. But he didn't stop even there. He wanted to be with us always, in the closest, most intimate union possible. He would give us his own flesh and blood to eat and drink, in the Eucharist. But first he had to prepare us for this gift, through a sign.

The preparation had begun a long, long time before. Almost thirteen centuries earlier, the Hebrews had found themselves short of food as their nomadic wanderings took them through a desert place. At that time they unexpectedly came upon a strange new kind of food which saved them from starvation. Seeing God's hand in this saving event, they called the food manna—bread from heaven. It was this event that the people may have remembered when Jesus fed them with the loaves and fish, and he reminds them of it as he promises the Eucharist.

When they came to him in great numbers the next day, he wasted no time getting to the point. He was almost harsh in his bluntness. "You've come to me because yesterday I gave you a free meal. You received food for nothing, and that impressed you. Look beyond the bread; it's only a sign. Expand your heart wishes. Widen your perspective. I have much greater things to give you."

Step by step he led them on. "Don't work for food that spoils; instead, work for food that lasts for eternal life. This is the food which the Son of Man will give you. . . ." They were eager now, and attentive. "Sir, give us this bread always."

And then he told them what he had been leading up to: "I am

the bread of life." He himself was to be their food and drink. His own flesh and blood would be their pledge of everlasting life.

That was when the prudent, sensible, calculating people took over. "What's that? His flesh and blood? How can he do that?" And the spell was broken. Pedestrian minds took over and brought everyone down to earth. Come, now, let's be reasonable. This is just too much to believe. You're not serious, are you?

If being popular was important to Jesus, it was clear what he should have done at that moment. If he didn't want to lose the crowd, he should have said something like this:

"Well, now, hold on, let's talk this over. I think we have a breakdown in communication here. Maybe you folks are taking me too literally. I didn't say you'll actually eat my flesh and drink my blood. No, I meant it like sort of a symbol. You know, . . . like when you eat the bread and drink the wine, you'd be reminded of me. A kind of memorial supper, if you know what I mean."

That's what he would have said, if PR had been his strong suit. Instead, he spells it out and nails it down:

Jesus said to them, "I am telling you the truth: if you do not eat the flesh of the Son of Man and drink his blood, you will not have life in yourselves."

That did it. The crowd left, and most of them never came back. They had eaten the loaves Christ multiplied the day before, but still they left. Jesus' Neilsen rating was never quite so high again. Instead of telling people what they want to hear, he tells them the truth. If they trust him, then maybe at a later time he can explain. If they don't trust him now, no matter how much of an explanation he gives, it won't make a bit of difference.

This, then, is the moment of truth, the moment of trust, the moment of the leap toward the other, the moment of adventure.

Many refuse the trust, the leap, the adventure—and go away.

Christ, discouraged, turns to the Twelve and asks, "And you— would you also like to leave?"

An awkward silence, and then Peter answers for the others. "Look, Lord, I'm terribly confused. I don't understand this at all. At the moment I don't know what this talk was all about. But I trust you. I've been with you now for some time. I know you've got it. I know you're from heaven. If we leave you, where are we going to go?"

Peter doesn't understand the Eucharist any better than the crowd did. It's just as mind-boggling for him. So what does he do?

His trust in Jesus overcomes the darkness and confusion of his mind. Instead of playing it safe, he takes the leap of faith, and brings the Eleven with him.

He can take you with him, too. All you have to do is say the words, "Lord, to whom would we go? You have the words that give eternal life." Say the words, and mean them.

Things to do

1. In multiplying the loaves and fish, Jesus was trying to prepare his followers for something. What was it? Why did he choose this way?
2. Of what event in their nation's history did this miracle remind the people?
3. The miraculous feeding on the hillside took place a very long time ago. How do we experience it in our own lives today?
4. One evening the crowd wanted to make him king. The next day they deserted him. How did Jesus' stock go up so fast and come down so fast? What does this tell you about him and about them?
5. When Jesus saw he was losing the crowd, why didn't he try to explain the mystery to them?
6. Do the apostles, who stay, understand Jesus' promise any more than the crowd, who leave? Why did they stay?
7. In your opinion, was Jesus too truthful for his own good?

The Woman at the Well

Jesus had to go through Samaria.

In Samaria he came to a town named Sychar, which was not far from the field that Jacob had given to his son Joseph. Jacob's well was there, and Jesus, tired out by the trip, sat down by the well. It was about noon.

A Samaritan woman came to draw some water, and Jesus said to her, "Give me a drink of water." (His disciples had gone into town to buy food.)

The woman answered, "You are a Jew, and I am a Samaritan —so how can you ask me for a drink?" (Jews will not use the same cups and bowls that Samaritans use.)

Jesus answered, "If you only knew what God gives and who it is that is asking you for a drink, you would ask him, and he would give you life-giving water."

"Sir," the woman said, "you don't have a bucket, and the well is deep. Where would you get that life-giving water? It was our ancestor Jacob who gave us this well; he and his sons and his flocks all drank from it. You don't claim to be greater than Jacob, do you?"

Jesus answered, "Whoever drinks this water will get thirsty again, but whoever drinks the water that I will give him will never be thirsty again. The water that I will give him will become in him a spring which will provide him with life-giving water and give him eternal life."

"Sir," the woman said, "give me that water! Then I will never be thirsty again, nor will I have to come here to draw water."

"Go and call your husband," Jesus told her, "and come back."

"I don't have a husband," she answered.

Jesus replied, "You are right when you say you don't have a husband.

"You have been married to five men, and the man you live with now is not really your husband. You have told me the truth."

"I see you are a prophet, sir," the woman said. "My Samaritan ancestors worshiped God on this mountain, but you Jews say that Jerusalem is the place where we should worship God."

Jesus said to her, "Believe me—woman, the time will come when people will not worship the Father either on this mountain or in Jerusalem. You Samaritans do not really know whom you worship; but we Jews know whom we worship, because it is from the Jews that salvation comes. But the time is coming and is already here, when by the power of God's Spirit people will worship the Father as he really is, offering him the true worship that he wants. God is Spirit, and only by the power of his Spirit can people worship him as he really is."

The woman said to him, "I know that the Messiah will come, and when he comes, he will tell us everything."

Jesus answered, "I am he, I who am talking with you."

At that moment Jesus' disciples returned, and they were greatly surprised to find him talking with a woman. But none of them said to her, "What do you want?" or asked him, "Why are you talking with her?"

Then the woman left her water jar, went back to the town, and said to the people there, "Come and see the man who told me everything I have ever done. Could he be the Messiah?" So they left the town and went to Jesus.

Many of the Samaritans in that town believed in Jesus because the woman had said, "He told me everything I have ever done." So when the Samaritans came to him, they begged him to stay with them, and Jesus stayed two days.

Many more believed because of his message, and they told the woman, "We believe now, not because of what you said, but because we ourselves have heard him, and we know that he really is the Savior of the world."—*John 4:4-30, 39-42*

"He told me everything I have ever done"

You can still get a drink from Jacob's well today. Just enter the charming little Greek Orthodox chapel that's built over the well and ask the priest to draw a cupful for you; he's very obliging. It's pure and fresh and delicious the way tap water could never be. When Jesus stopped there, of course, there was no chapel. The noonday sun was merciless, and he was probably very thirsty. But he was looking for something more than water when he asked the Samaritan woman for a drink.

She must have wondered what he was after. She was a well-used woman who had been around the league a few times and was used to men asking her for favors. Was this another one? After all she'd seen, it was pretty hard to shake her up; there weren't many surprises left for her. Even so, she didn't expect a Jew to talk to her. There was so much bad feeling between Samaritans and Jews in those days that they avoided each other's turf as much as possible and frowned on all social contact. Jews passing through Samaria usually traveled in large groups in case there might be a rumble. This woman, who had broken most of the taboos in her society, was still a bit uptight when Jesus broke this one. "You are a Jew, and I am a Samaritan—so how can you ask me for a drink?"

The way he answers makes her even more curious. If she knew who he was, he says, she would have asked him for living water and he would have given it to her. Is he serious? Or is he another fast talker with a smooth line? (She knows all about *that* kind.) So she plays it straight and goes along with him. "You don't have a rope and pail to draw water. How would you get it?" But instead of clearing up this strange little conversation, he gets even more mysterious. "Whoever drinks this water will get thirsty again, but whoever drinks the water that I will give him will never be thirsty again."

He's talking in riddles. And she wonders: is he putting me on? But there's something about him that makes her pause. He's not like the other men she's known. This one looks honest, and there's a quiet strength about him. I feel as though I have to take him seriously, because . . . well, he takes *me* seriously. So, instead of a wisecrack, she's surprised to hear herself say, "Sir, give me that water!"

His reply is disconcerting. "Go, and call your husband, and come back." And when she replies that she has no husband, he makes

the most astounding statement yet: "You are right when you say you don't have a husband. You have been married to five men, and the man you live with now is not really your husband."

Now that was a sneaky blow! So that's what he was leading up to! But how did he know? Who is this stranger, anyway? And why am I letting him talk to me this way?

But she doesn't turn him off; instead, she tries to change the subject. Let's talk about religion; it's a lot less threatening topic than my love life. How about the long-standing dispute about the Temple? The Jews say it belongs in Jerusalem where it is; we Samaritans say it should be here, on this mountain. Jesus goes along with her, more or less. He'll talk religion, but he makes it clear that the question of worshipping God is a lot bigger than Jerusalem or Samaria, and that very soon this intramural argument will be obsolete. Does he mean the Messianic age is near, as many Jews and Samaritans believe and hope? The Messiah, she says, will teach us these things. And she can hardly believe her ears when he comes up with one last bombshell: "I am he."

If anyone else had said that, she would have laughed and called him crazy. But this man isn't crazy, and he's not one to be laughed at.

What a time for his disciples to come back! There was so much she wanted to ask him, but she couldn't talk while they were there. So she ran back into town, even forgetting the water she had come for, and told everybody she met about the remarkable stranger. You can't help wondering why anyone paid any attention to her. She wasn't a respectable person. Many must have looked down on her for her bohemian life-style. She wasn't much different from a prostitute. If there's going to be a religious happening, you don't expect it from *her*.

And yet there was something about her that made them stop and listen and then want to go see for themselves. She looked different today; she had had an experience that transformed her, even in the eyes of her friends and neighbors.

He told me everything I have ever done. That's the expression that occurs more than once in this unusual conversion story. It stayed with her long after she'd forgotten what they'd said about temples and worship and theology. For he had known all about her . . . or rather, he knew *her*. And in telling her what he knew about her, a strange thing happened: she came to see herself the way she never had before. For years she'd been hiding from herself. She'd gone from one man to another so quickly and easily that sometimes their

33

names and faces got mixed up in her mind. Worse still, she was getting fuzzy about who *she* was. Until this man spoke to her today.

He told me everything I have ever done. Didn't she know what she had done? Why did she need him to tell her? Because sin is alienation. To be a sinner is to lose touch with our real self . . . to accept the roles thrust upon us by others, to live up to other people's expectations instead of our own ideals, to surrender our values in exchange for some glittering bauble that shines in our eyes and blinds us to what's good and true. She had a lot of practice in covering up the truth from herself. She hadn't really looked in a mirror for years, until he made her do it. When he did, she didn't like what she saw, but somehow he made it bearable. Others had told her off before, in plain blunt terms. But this wasn't just another put-down. He seemed really to care about her, and he gave her the feeling that she could be different. Was it because he believed in her more than she believed in herself?

People who get involved with Jesus Christ often have the same basic experience as the Samaritan woman. When I study him, listen to his words and take them to heart, I find myself living at a different level of awareness. I get beyond the noise and beneath the surface to the real me. It's like when he traveled through Galilee and Judea. When he was around, the masks came off. And those who wanted to keep their masks on stayed away. To some, the masks were so important that they would stop at nothing to keep them, even if it meant killing him.

Most people aren't anxious to know themselves the way God knows them. Most would rather live on the surface and settle for blurred and fuzzy images of themselves. It's safer that way. If I never really know myself I'll never have to change anything. I can substitute routine for realization and avoid all the sweat that goes with becoming a real person.

Let's face it. When the Samaritan woman encountered Jesus and allowed him to get through to her, her life became complicated. Some things could never be the same again. She might have to give up some of her most cherished kicks. Changes would have to be made. Where did she get the courage? From him, of course.

If you want to play it cozy and achieve the goal of undisturbed mediocrity, don't get too involved with Christianity. A little surface religiosity is okay, but keep your cool and avoid the deep stuff. Encounters with Jesus are dangerous. They can reveal us to ourselves and make us dissatisfied with compromise. They can infect us with idealism and lead us on to high and noble resolves. They can even damage the crust of selfishness that surrounds our heart and protects us from sacrifice. What happened to the Samaritan woman could happen to us. We might start to live.

Things to do

1. Why did Jews and Samaritans hate one another so much?
2. In this encounter, did the woman learn more about God, or about herself? Does this tell you anything about the nature of religious experience?
3. Until she met Jesus, what kept the woman's real self hidden from her? Why did she have to meet him to find herself?
4. Compare Jesus' reception in this hostile town of foreigners with his experience in his home town of Nazareth. The latter story is in the fourth chapter of Luke's Gospel. How would you explain the contrast?
5. Have you ever had an experience of self-awareness like this woman's? Would you care to tell us about it?
6. Was she really better off for having met Jesus? Didn't he create more problems for her than he solved?
7. If you wanted to have an experience like this, how would you go about it?

The Final Journey

The Final Journey

As the opposition hardened and the circle of Jesus' friends grew smaller, he saw the clouds gathering and knew the storm must break very soon. He was on a collision course with the religious authorities, with whom a decisive confrontation could no longer be avoided. The crowds, though still fascinated by Jesus and subject to occasional bursts of enthusiasm, were clearly too fickle and unreliable to be counted on in the crunch. He knew that if push came to shove, they would either desert him or turn on him.

This left his inner circle of followers, still loyal to him but hopelessly muddled about him and the true nature of his mission. In the face of his clear denials, they persisted in fantasizing about an imminent upheaval, a social and political revolution with him at the head and them close behind. The longer they lived on these illusions, the more total would be their downfall when disaster struck. The time had come for plain talk, and it began outside a little town called Caesarea Philippi. . . .

The Profession of Peter

Jesus went to the territory near the town of Caesarea Philippi, where he asked his disciples, "Who do people say the Son of Man is?"

"Some say John the Baptist," they answered. "Others say Elijah, while others say Jeremiah or some other prophet."

"What about you?" he asked them. "Who do you say I am?"

Simon Peter answered, "You are the Messiah, the Son of the living God."

"Good for you, Simon son of John!" answered Jesus. "For this truth did not come to you from any human being, but it was given to you directly by my Father in heaven. And so I tell you, Peter: you are a rock, and on this rock foundation I will build my church, and not even death will ever be able to overcome it. I will give you the keys of the Kingdom of heaven; what you prohibit on earth will be prohibited in heaven, and what you permit on earth will be permitted in heaven." —*Matthew 16:13-19*

"Who do you say that I am?"

If there's a turning point in the public life of Christ, it's the conversation at Caesarea Philippi between Jesus and his closest followers. The disciples didn't know what Jesus knew—that he was about to launch his last drive on Jerusalem. This Passover celebration will be his last, for the price of confrontation with Judea's religious leaders will be his own death.

As he prepared for this final showdown, he was painfully aware that his followers were in no way ready for the fatal struggle. All his efforts to educate them seemed to have failed. No matter how he tried to divert them, they persisted in thinking that they were to be at the cutting edge of some social or political revolution that would transform Jewish society. They were utterly unprepared to grasp the spiritual nature of the kingdom. And the means of establishing that kingdom—Jesus' humiliation and murder—would be incomprehensible.

The time for teaching is running out. He must tell them, in brutally plain language, what's going to happen. But first he must elicit an act of faith in himself, to carry them through the darkest hours of failure and disillusionment.

Perhaps it was after a meal on the road, while they were all together resting before the next journey. Like a candidate asking the results of the latest poll, he asks them: "Who do people say the Son of Man is?" This is not the important question, but it will do for starters. The answers come quickly. "Some say John the Baptist." "Others say Elijah, while others say Jeremiah or some other prophet."

Now for the big one.

"What about you? Who do *you* say that I am?"

They looked at one another. Something in the way he asked the question told them that this was a serious moment. He was not asking for a routine report now. He wanted to know where they stood. Why were they following him? What was the basis for their relationship? What did he mean to them?

Simon Peter was the first to find words for the deep feelings that stirred within them. Speaking for them all, he made that magnificent profession of faith: "You are the Messiah, the Son of the living God."

A pregnant silence followed, as Jesus looked around the group. In each man's eyes he read the wordless message: Yes, that goes for me. They had made the leap of trust and staked all on him and his word. They didn't grasp what he was about, but they grasped who he was. That's all he could expect for now, but it was enough to build on.

"Good for you, Simon son of John!" answered Jesus. "For this truth did not come to you from any human being, but it was given to you directly by my Father in heaven."

To recognize Jesus for what he is, and to make an act of faith in him, takes more than brains or education. It takes a revelation from God himself. Simon received that revelation and responded in faith, not because he was smarter or a better person than others, but because he was open to Jesus and gave God's grace a chance. In a word, he was offered the gift of faith and didn't turn it down. And that made all the difference. It made him a new man, and Jesus underlines this by giving him a new name:

"And so I tell you, Peter: you are a rock, and on this rock foundation I will build my church, and not even death will ever be able to overcome it. I will give you the keys of the Kingdom of heaven."

Peter and the Eleven, who have made the leap of faith, are to be the foundation stones of the New Order.

In some ways it was a weak foundation. The Twelve were uneducated, without political power or influence, fuzzy and confused even about what their own leader had in mind. But there were strong points, too. They were idealistic, they wanted to do great things, they wanted to serve. Most important of all, they were personally committed to Jesus Christ. They had acknowledged him as their leader and savior and had freely chosen to follow him wherever he might lead. They had almost no appreciation of what was involved, and this was going to cost them dearly in the tragic weeks ahead. But this personal commitment was ultimately going to see them through.

One of the most striking things about Jesus is this feeling he creates in people that they must make a decision about him. In his lifetime very few people were neutral on the subject of Jesus of Nazareth. Most were either for him or against him, and that was the way he wanted it. There have always been those who tried to study him at a distance and keep it theoretical, but it's difficult if you listen to him and take him seriously. If he were just another philosopher with a theory on what life is all about, it would be easier to avoid taking a stand. We could accept some of his ideas and reject others. But it wasn't a philosophy that he offered us; it was himself. He didn't force himself on people, but he provoked and challenged them to take a stand in his regard.

Many, especially in our day, have tried to picture Jesus as an uncomplicated humanist promoting a simple message of love and non-violence, uninterested in questions of God or religion. He becomes the equal of Socrates or Buddha or Gandhi, but nothing more. For them, the question of Jesus' divine sonship is a distraction. If they're right, it's hard to understand why he aroused such extremes of loyalty and hatred, and even harder to figure out why he got killed. Time and time again, on almost every page of the New Testament, we find him asking, in one way or another, the question he put to the Twelve at Caesarea Philippi: Who do you say that I am? For those who believed in him, the possibilities were unlimited. For those who didn't, Jesus couldn't make much happen.

How about you? Who do *you* say that he is?

Things to do

1. In what sense was the Caesarea Philippi incident a turning point in Jesus' public life?
2. How did this encounter affect the relationship between Jesus and his men?
3. How could the apostles be so close to Jesus and yet not grasp what he was trying to do?
4. What does Jesus mean when he says to Peter, ". . . this truth did not come to you from any human being"?
5. What is the significance of his change of name from Simon to Peter?
6. "They had almost no appreciation of what was involved, and this was going to cost them dearly in the weeks ahead." How did this work out?
7. Jesus once said, "He who is not with me is against me." Why is it so difficult to study Jesus like any other philosopher? Why do so many people feel they have to take a stand about him, one way or the other?
8. This happened to one of the authors of this book several years ago. A high school senior, after taking a course on Jesus, said he could not yet give a personal answer to Christ's question, "Who do you say that I am?" And he didn't know what to do.

    Do you think he was copping out?

    What would you say to him?

Prediction of the Passion

From that time on Jesus began to say plainly to his disciples, "I must go to Jerusalem and suffer much from the elders, the chief priests, and the teachers of the Law. I will be put to death, but three days later I will be raised to life."

Peter took him aside and began to rebuke him. "God forbid it, Lord!" he said. "That must never happen to you!"

Jesus turned around and said to Peter, "Get away from me, Satan! You are an obstacle in my way, because these thoughts of yours don't come from God, but from man."

Then Jesus said to his disciples, "If anyone wants to come with me, he must forget himself, carry his cross, and follow me. For whoever wants to save his own life will lose it; but whoever loses his life for my sake will find it. Will a person gain anything if he wins the whole world but loses his life? Of course not! There is nothing he can give to regain his life. For the Son of Man is about to come in the glory of his Father with his angels, and then he will repay everyone according to his deeds." —*Matthew 16:21-27*

"Get away from me, Satan!"

Once Peter and the others had made their profession of faith in Jesus as the Messiah, it was time for Jesus to make his move. He must go to Jerusalem for the final struggle. But first he will tell them precisely what's in store for them if they make this last journey with him.

"From that time on Jesus began to say plainly to his disciples, 'I must go to Jerusalem and suffer much from the elders, the chief priests, and the teachers of the Law. I will be put to death, but three days later I will be raised to life.' "

Did Jesus have miraculous knowledge of the future? Or was he simply spelling out the dangers involved in visiting Jerusalem at this time, when plots against his life were common knowledge? We don't know for sure. At any rate, he couldn't have been more explicit in pointing out the cost of discipleship. He told it like it was . . . and would be.

What was the effect? Well, Peter has just been designated the leader of the group, so he tries to take charge. He takes Jesus aside and gives him a friendly piece of advice. This is no way to talk to your followers. It's bad for their morale. And we'd never let it happen anyway. So please—no more talk of suffering and dying; it doesn't help anybody.

Peter meant well. The thought of Jesus getting killed was unbearable and made no sense to him. He was a devoted, success-oriented follower, so he spoke from the heart when he urged his master to be more optimistic. So he was dumbfounded when Jesus turned and lashed out at him: "Get away from me, you devil! You're in my way. You're not on the side of God, but of men!"

This is how Jesus talks to the man who, moments ago, was designated the rock on which he would build his Church. One minute Peter is raised to the heights, the next he's sternly denounced as a traitor. Just because he didn't want to hear of his master's suffering and death. At that moment Peter realized that he didn't know Jesus nearly as well as he had thought. People who read this passage for the first time often get the same feeling.

When we read this account today, we have the advantage of knowing why Jesus reacted so strongly to Peter's suggestion. We know that the cross was inevitable, that Christ had to save us by his death and resurrection. So we're inclined to feel a bit superior, as though we're clued in while Peter and the others are in the dark. But are we, really? Do we understand the Cross? More important, do we *accept* it? How do you feel about suffering? Is it the one big no-no that must be avoided at all cost? If you feel that way, you have a lot of people for company, but Jesus isn't among them.

There's one more thing to note about Peter's reaction to Jesus' prediction of his fate. Did you notice what he missed? He heard Jesus speak of suffering and death, and he didn't like what he heard, and said so. But that wasn't the whole story foretold by Jesus. He also said he would rise again the third day, but by that time Peter couldn't hear, because he had stopped listening.

Did you miss it, too? It's easy to do. Suffering and death are frightening realities, and all our instincts rebel against them, so that when they present themselves we turn off our minds. And so, like Peter, we fail to hear what Jesus is trying to tell us. He was talking to *us,* as well as to the Twelve, when he told them:

"If anyone wants to come with me, he must carry his cross, and follow me." Terrifying words! But listen to what comes next:

"Will a person gain anything if he wins the whole world but loses his life? Of course not! There is nothing he can give to regain his life." It's a hard saying, but Jesus tells us, in no uncertain terms, that if we try to escape the Cross we'll lose everything. And then the supreme paradox: Only if we're ready to lose our lives can we hope to save them. The words would be impenetrable, if we didn't know Jesus crucified and risen from the dead. If we can believe in him and his promise, we won't find suffering and death easy to accept, but we'll be able to accept his offer of grace and its guarantee of victory.

If you feel overwhelmed by all this, don't be discouraged. The first time he said it to his followers, it went right over their heads. They just weren't ready. But the patient Christ could wait for them, as he waits for us.

Things to do
1. Jesus' reaction to Peter's well-meant advice is so violent. Do you think he felt threatened? Why?
2. Does an expression like "take up your cross" have the same impact on us today as it did on the disciples of that time? Explore the historical and cultural factors in our environment and theirs that would account for the difference.
3. Do you think today's American culture makes it easier or harder

for us to accept the doctrine of the Cross? Explain.
4. Explore the world of advertising for evidence to support your answer to #3.
5. Why did Peter and the others ignore completely what Jesus said about resurrection?
6. Let each student in the class bring at least one crucifix or picture of Christ crucified to school. Compare the ways he is depicted; which do you prefer?

You may find that some crucifixes portray Jesus in agony, with brutal realism. Most picture him as suffering, but in an idealized, less-shocking way. Others portray him as a glorious king reigning in triumph. Which style is "right"? Why? If you were a pastor building a church, which kind would you put over the altar?

The Transfiguration

Six days later Jesus took with him Peter and the brothers James and John and led them up a high mountain where they were alone. As they looked on, a change came over Jesus: his face was shining like the sun, and his clothes were dazzling white. Then the three disciples saw Moses and Elijah talking with Jesus, "Lord, how good it is that we are here! If you wish, I will make three tents here, one for you, one for Moses, and one for Elijah."

While he was talking, a shining cloud came over them, and a voice from the cloud said, "This is my own dear Son, with whom I am pleased—listen to him!"

When the disciples heard the voice, they were so terrified that they threw themselves face downward on the ground. Jesus came to them and touched them. "Get up," he said. "Don't be afraid!" So they looked up and saw no one there but Jesus.

As they came down the mountain, Jesus ordered them, "Don't tell anyone about this vision you have seen until the Son of Man has been raised from death." —*Matthew 17:1-9*

"Get up. Don't be afraid!"

Jesus' first prediction of his suffering and death, and his attempt to put it into perspective for his followers, was a failure. He had made them worried and anxious, but they were afraid to discuss the matter with him. It was like a cloud that wouldn't go away; they could only make believe it wasn't there.

But he couldn't leave it alone. The showdown was getting closer, and he had to give them something to hold onto when the going got rough. So he took the same three men—Peter, James, and John—who would later be with him during his agony in the garden of Gethsemane. In Gethsemane they would see him at his lowest point, when fear and loathing and loneliness would render him help-less and almost crush him. But now, for a few unforgettable mo-ments, it would be different. He took them to the lonely summit of a mountain, where in his presence they had a kind of mystical religious experience that would stay with them for the rest of their lives.

What was the meaning of those dreamlike moments when they were carried out of themselves, when time seemed to stand still and the tangible, workaday world ceased to be? Years later, Peter would write to his fellow Christians,

> We have not depended on made-up stories in making known to you the mighty coming of our Lord Jesus Christ. With our own eyes we saw his greatness. We were there when he was given honor and glory by God the Father, when the voice came to him from the Supreme Glory, say-ing, "This is my own dear Son, with whom I am pleased!" We ourselves heard this voice coming from heaven, when we were with him on the holy mountain. —*2 Peter 1:16-18*

The memory of those moments on the mountain never left him or his companions. It was a source of strength to them, and that was what Jesus meant it to be. For a brief time the divinity shone through, and he was no longer the down-to-earth, everyday Jesus who walked and ate and slept beside them. In a sense he always stood out from the crowd, for he was no ordinary man. But make no mistake: when God became one of us, he went all the way. He didn't just *seem* hu-man; he was a human being in the fullest sense of the term, just like you and me. In a way, the marvel wasn't that he looked the way he did in those ecstatic moments on the mountain, but that he didn't *always* look that way. This is what St. Paul meant when he wrote to the community at Philippi about Jesus:

> He always had the nature of God, but he did not think that by force he should try to become equal with God. Instead of this, of his own free will he gave up all he had, and took the nature of a servant. He became like man and appeared in human likeness. He was humble and walked the path of obedience all the way to death—his death on the cross. —*Philippians 2:6-8*

But for these few moments he gives his friends a glimpse of who he is. And they're carried completely out of themselves. Peter doesn't want the moment to end. Like someone trying to hold onto a beautiful dream, he begins babbling incoherently: "Let's make three tents here, one for you, one for Moses, and one for Elijah." He wants to stop the world and stay here, like this, forever. But even as he rambles on, the scene comes to a thunderous climax, as the cloud envelops them and the voice of God is heard: "This is my own dear Son . . . listen to him!" And they fell on their faces in fear and awe.

Later they would recall the account of that other occasion when Moses and their fathers met God on another mountain:

> On the morning of the third day there was thunder and lightning, a thick cloud appeared on the mountain, and a very loud trumpet blast was heard. All the people in the camp trembled with fear. Moses led them out of the camp to meet God, and they stood at the foot of the mountain. All of Mount Sinai was covered with smoke, because the LORD had come down on it in fire. The smoke went up like the smoke of a furnace, and all the people trembled violently. The sound of the trumpet became louder and louder. Moses spoke, and God answered him with thunder. The LORD came down on the top of Mount Sinai and called Moses to the top of the mountain. Moses went up. . . . —*Exodus 19:16-20*

How long they remained prostrate and trembling on the ground they couldn't say. Was it like our dreams, that seem so long but last only for seconds? At any rate, it was over as suddenly as it had begun. The next thing they knew, the cloud and the voice were gone, and Jesus was shaking them, telling them to get up. "Get up. Don't be afraid." When they looked up, everything was as before the vision.

Jesus was alone, looking as he always did. And so, like men emerging from a trance, they came back to reality. Or was it the other way around?

Jesus gave his close friends a glimpse of his glory to help them through the hard times he knew were ahead for them. He still does this sometimes, for us. Most of us have known peak moments, when God seemed very real and close and the spiritual world felt as real as the world of sight and sound and touch. It may be at a Eucharist with our friends, when praying comes easily, when everything—music, people, gestures—seems to fit. Or it may come in moments of quiet, when we're alone without being lonely. A sunset or a flower or a deserted beach can bring on these special times when we feel in touch with ourselves and with the One who made us. Do you know what we mean?

These special moments are a blessing, but they're out of the ordinary. (That's why they're special.) Most of the time, we have to plod along without visions, without peak experiences, without even a warm feeling. That's why following Christ is different from being in a parade, and Palm Sunday was a one-shot spectacular. So was the transfiguration on the mountain. Like the apostles when they came back to earth, we look around and see nothing out of the ordinary. Only Jesus is there, beckoning us to follow him on rainy days as well as on sunny ones. He made many promises, but one promise he never got around to making. He forgot to guarantee that we would never be bored.

Can you worship when you don't feel like it? Do you ever pray even when you're not in the mood? Are you kind to clods and gentle with fools? These are the times that try our souls, when sunshine patriots fall away. How about you? Are you with Christ only on mountain tops? Most of the action is in the valley.

Things to do
1. Why did the disciples need an experience like this?
2. Have you ever had a peak religious moment? What brought it on, and what was it like?
3. Many people today seem to have little tolerance for boredom or routine in religious activities. In looking for "highs" and emotional satisfaction, do you think they have unrealistic expectations?
4. If church isn't exciting, why go to church?
5. Is the quality of a relationship best perceived in good times, or in periods of stress? Back up your answer with examples.

Cure of the Epileptic Boy

When they joined the rest of the disciples, they saw a large crowd around them and some teachers of the Law arguing with them. When the people saw Jesus, they were greatly surprised, and ran to him and greeted him. Jesus asked his disciples, "What are you arguing with them about?"

A man in the crowd answered, "Teacher, I brought my son to you, because he has an evil spirit in him and cannot talk. Whenever the spirit attacks him, it throws him to the ground, and he foams at the mouth, grits his teeth, and becomes stiff all over. I asked your disciples to drive the spirit out, but they could not."

Jesus said to them, "How unbelieving you people are! How long must I stay with you? How long do I have to put up with you? Bring the boy to me!" They brought him to Jesus.

As soon as the spirit saw Jesus, it threw the boy into a fit, so that he fell on the ground and rolled around, foaming at the mouth. "How long has he been like this?" Jesus asked the father.

"Ever since he was a child," he replied. "Many times the evil spirit has tried to kill him by throwing him in the fire and into water. Have pity on us and help us, if you possibly can!"

"Yes," said Jesus, "if you yourself can! Everything is possible for the person who has faith."

The father at once cried out, "I do have faith, but not enough. Help me have more!"

Jesus noticed that the crowd was closing in on them, so he gave a command to the evil spirit. "Deaf and dumb spirit," he said, "I order you to come out of the boy and never go into him again!"

The spirit screamed, threw the boy into a bad fit, and came out. The boy looked like a corpse and everyone said, "He is dead!" But Jesus took the boy by the hand and helped him rise, and he stood up.
—Mark 9:14-27

Help!

When Jesus and his three companions came down from the mount of transfiguration and rejoined the other disciples, they came upon a scene of anxiety and confusion. During their absence, a man had brought his sick boy to the disciples and asked them to cure him. They often received such requests, and in the past had helped many, but this time they couldn't do anything. This left the father disappointed and their confidence shaken. There was embarrassment mixed with relief when Jesus appeared.

The father, in desperation, rushes up to get help for his son, who seems to be suffering from epilepsy. His anxiety brings a note of reproach into his voice: "I asked your men to help, and they couldn't."

It doesn't happen often, but occasionally we get a glimpse of a side of Jesus that rarely appeared. He could get fed up with the people around him. His usual reaction to their pettiness, their unreasonable demands, and lack of consideration was a monumental patience. But every once in a long while the exasperation would come through, and he'd tell them off. This was one of those times. As he looked round the group, he read the skepticism and the doubt in their eyes. Never mind the signs, the good works, the cures till now, they seemed to say; what have you done for us lately? So he lets them have it: "How unbelieving you people are! How long do I have to put up with you?"

But his annoyance wouldn't stand in the way of his compassion. So he calls for the boy, who at this moment falls into a convulsion. The boy begins to roll around and foam at the mouth.

Christ appears to ignore the boy and asks a question that sounds like someone with all the time in the world filling out a medical form. The father is beside himself. "Help us, if you possibly can!" Still Christ appears to ignore the boy rolling on the ground, and begins another discussion.

The poor man has had it. In his grief and frustration he's hit bottom. He hardly knows where he is.

"You ask me if I believe; you ask me if I trust. I don't know if I believe or not. I don't know if I trust or not. I just don't know. I can't do anything by myself anymore.

"I think I'm trying to believe. Help my unbelief! I think I'm trying to trust. Help me to trust! . . . Help!"

This man was at a rock-bottom crisis. His only prayer—he doesn't even know if it is a prayer—is "Help!"

And that was enough. It was all that Jesus wanted to hear. He cures the boy, and gives him back to his father.

Most of us, at one time or another, find the boy's father a very easy guy to identify with. Consider his predicament and see if it doesn't sound familiar. He's at the end of his rope and needs help that only Jesus can give. But, as we see over and over again, Jesus can't help people unless they have faith in him. It wasn't just his enemies and his critics that he couldn't do anything for; the skeptics and the fence-sitters were disqualified, too. Without trust, nothing could happen. So what was the father to do? He couldn't just pretend to have faith; that would have been dishonest. It would have been phony to say things he didn't mean. Sure, he *wished* and *hoped* that Christ would help, but he didn't *know*. He just wasn't sure. But neither could he just walk away, for that would have meant giving up on his own son, whose health depended on a faith the father couldn't feel.

If you ever find yourself in a situation like this, it's comforting to know that Jesus accepted the father's prayer, which wasn't an act of faith but simply a request for faith. You see, anybody can *ask* for faith. Maybe you find it hard to believe (don't we all, sometimes?), but there's nothing to stop you from asking for the gift of faith. It takes just one syllable to cry "Help!" What's the big deal?

Remember this prayer, and file it away for future reference: "Lord, I'm trying to believe. Help my unbelief!" It may come in handy some day if you ever hit rock bottom. When you hear the scraping sound, it's time for what may be the best prayer you ever said.

Things to do

1. Why was it difficult for the boy's father to trust in Jesus' ability to cure him?
2. Why did Jesus lose his temper?
3. It's evident from this account that the health of the boy ultimately depended on his father's ability to make some kind of act of faith in Jesus. Does this seem right? What does it tell us about the way God deals with people?
4. Have you ever been in a predicament like the father's? How did you handle it? What would you do next time?

PART III

Tragedy and Triumph

Tragedy and Triumph

Time had run out; the hour of decision had struck. Jesus and his followers were entering Jerusalem with the throngs of pilgrims gathered from all over the Mediterranean world for the Passover. The city was in a fever of expectation. Pontius Pilate, the Roman governor in charge of the foreign occupation forces, was taking the usual precautions against the kind of popular uprising that was always a possibility during this religious festival.

A spontaneous demonstration sprang up around the figure of Jesus, as the people waved palm branches and escorted him into the city in a kind of triumphal march. There was no violence, so the Romans took no notice; but the religious leaders watched—and didn't like what they saw. They resolved to discredit him, and for the next few days tried to trap him in religious controversy. But he turned back every attack and humiliated them in front of the people. So they decided that the only way to dispose of him and the threat he posed was to kill him.

Their chance came from an unexpected quarter. Judas came to them and offered to betray Jesus into their hands. Now the security of Jesus' inner circle could be broken. For thirty pieces of silver, they had a deal.

This was the situation on Thursday night, when Jesus and his disciples gathered to eat what they called the Passover meal and which would be known to history as the Last Supper.

The Lord's Supper: Washing of the Feet

It was now the day before the Passover Festival. Jesus knew that the hour had come for him to leave this world and go to the Father. He had always loved those in the world who were his own, and he loved them to the very end.

Jesus and his disciples were at supper. The Devil had already put the thought of betraying Jesus into the heart of Judas, the son of Simon Iscariot. Jesus knew that the Father had given him complete power; he knew that he had come from God and was going to God. So he rose from the table, took off his outer garment, and tied a towel around his waist. Then he poured some water into a washbasin and began to wash the disciples' feet and dry them with the towel around his waist. He came to Simon Peter, who said to him, "Are you going to wash my feet, Lord?"

Jesus answered him, "You do not understand now what I am doing, but you will understand later."

Peter declared, "Never at any time will you wash my feet!"

"If I do not wash your feet," Jesus answered, "you will no longer be my disciple."

Simon Peter answered, "Lord, do not wash only my feet, then! Wash my hands and head, too!"

After Jesus had washed their feet, he put his outer garment back on and returned to his place at the table. "Do you understand what I have just done to you?" he asked. "You call me Teacher and Lord, and it is right that you do so, because that is what I am. I, your Lord and Teacher, have just washed your feet. You, then, should wash one another's feet. I have set an example for you, so that you will do just what I have done for you.

"And now I give you a new commandment: love one another. As I have loved you, so you must love one another. If you have love for one another, then everyone will know that you are my disciples."
—*John 13:1-9, 12-15, 34-35*

"You will understand later"

The fateful hour had arrived. Jesus had a few hours of freedom left, a few more hours of life. His disciples weren't ready for this final struggle; all his efforts to prepare them had failed. Now he would take his last meal with them, his Last Supper. Every word, every gesture was charged with special meaning which only he could grasp now; they would come to understand much later.

The first gesture, which surprised and troubled them, was the washing of the feet. It was customary at that time that when a guest came to the house a servant would wash the dust from his feet. The servant who was the low man on the totem pole must have been the one who got stuck with this job.

The disciples are amazed when Jesus takes on this lowly task, and good old impetuous Peter manages to put his foot in it again.

"No, sir," says Peter, "you're not going to wash *my* feet."

"Look," says Christ, "this is very important. Don't get stubborn."

Peter says, "Lord, I'm a dummy. Wash my feet—and you better wash this thick head of mine while you're at it."

After washing the disciples' feet, Christ returns to the table. "Do you understand what this is all about? I've given you a sign of love. I've given you an example of love. I've been giving you love for the last couple of years. I want you to love one another the way I love you."

One of the pairs of feet belonged to Judas, the man who had sold him out to his enemies. What went through the minds of Jesus and Judas at that moment? Was Jesus making one last attempt to move that stony heart? Did Judas feel a twinge of shame at receiving this mark of deference from the master he had betrayed? We'll never know. But one thing we do know: the love that Jesus Christ has for sinners is something very special. Most of us, no matter how easygoing or thick-skinned we are, put limits on how forgiving we will be. That's just one of the differences between us and the Savior of the world. It's even harder to forgive those who've been close to us. For a couple of years Judas lived very close to Jesus. They traveled, ate, and slept in each other's company. They had shared secrets, confided in each other, gone through good times and bad together.

And now it has come to this: Judas is a traitor, and the man he betrayed is washing his feet.

There are two messages here for us—an encouragement, and a warning. No matter what I've done, no matter how badly I've messed up, Christ believes in me and sees possibilities when everyone else (including myself) has given up on me. No matter how badly or how often I've let him down, he reaches out to me in forgiveness and love. If he can wash the feet of Judas, he can put up with me.

But this doesn't mean I can take him for granted. If I resist his grace and persist in my selfishness or dishonesty or cruelty, I run the risk of pushing myself over the line, past the point of no return, where he can no longer reach me. That's what happened to Judas, who was once very close to Christ, one of his inner circle of intimate friends. And if it could happen to him, it could happen to anyone, including me. Not that Jesus gives up on anyone; he never does. But any relationship can die when one of the parties hardens his or her heart and makes reconciliation impossible. If the tragedy of Judas tells us anything, it tells us that even the limitless love of Christ can be turned off forever by the human heart.

The Lord's Supper: Institution of the Eucharist

Then he took a piece of bread, gave thanks to God, broke it, and gave it to them, saying, "This is my body, which is given for you. Do this in memory of me." In the same way, he gave them the cup after the supper, saying, "This cup is God's new covenant sealed with my blood, which is poured out for you."—*Luke 22:19-20*

"This is my body"

A marvelous thing then happened. Christ took bread, gave it to those who were with him and said, "This is my body." After eating he did the same with the cup and said, "This cup is God's new covenant sealed with my blood." He told those with him to do this also in the future as a remembrance of him.

To a certain extent the apostles understood at that time what was happening. But it was only later, under the influence of the Holy Spirit, that they began to grasp its full significance. In fact, throughout their lives they had a deeper and deeper experience of it.

Why did Jesus give us the Eucharist? Because he wants to be with us. When you love someone very much, you want to be with that person and share your life with him or her. When God became man in Jesus Christ and died for us, it seemed that he could do no more to show his love. But he went even further. He found a way to be with us always, to be our very food under the form of bread and wine. That's what *com-union* means—being joined in a union too intimate and astounding for our minds to grasp.

If it had happened just once in the history of the world that the Son of God gave himself to human beings this way, it would be a wonderful thing. But this isn't something that took place just once, at a certain time in a certain place. It happens today, every day, whenever Christians meet to celebrate the Eucharist. When priest and people join in the Mass, Christ becomes truly present on the altar and gives himself to us as he gave himself to the apostles on the first Holy Thursday. In Holy Communion he is as close to us as he was to his little band of followers in the supper room that fateful night.

Catholics often complain and argue about the Mass. They complain about the sermons and the music. They argue about whether they should have to attend every Sunday. "Why can't I stay home and talk to God?" is a question often asked. Some young people say it's a bore . . . "like an old rerun on TV," said one student.

These are real problems that are important to a lot of people, and we can't just dismiss them. How do we answer them? Well, start at the beginning. The Eucharist was never intended to be entertaining or to compete with television or rock concerts. It's a sacred action at the heart of our religion, in which God gives himself to us his people. If that isn't important to me, then the most eloquent sermons, the best music, and the grooviest gathering of the most beautiful people won't turn me on.

Sure, the priest should try to preach well. The choir should practice. The planning and participation in the liturgy are important. But even when these are uninspired . . . and it's hard to be inspiring every week . . . we must remember the heart of the matter. Jesus Christ, the Son of God, is right here in our midst, and he wants to be united with me and with those around me. Some people think the friendship of Christ is so important that they find it hard to be bored at the Eucharist, and if the boredom happens, they can put up with it. That's the way it is with the most important relationships in our lives: they can survive boredom, can rise above dullness and routine.

Things to do
1. What was Jesus trying to accomplish by the washing of the feet?
2. Do you think it was hard for Jesus to wash Judas' feet?
3. How could Judas be so close to Jesus for so long and end up this way?
4. Since nearly everybody is keeping his shoes on these days, how can we fulfill the Lord's command to wash one another's feet? (Try to get beyond generalities to specifics: at school, at home, etc.)
5. Do you think the Eucharist can mean anything to a person who doesn't have a personal relationship with Jesus?
6. If we had this relationship, would most of our problems with the Mass be solved?
7. Have you ever had a relationship that survived boredom and routine?

Agony in the Garden

Then Jesus went with his disciples to a place called Gethsemane and he said to them, "Sit here while I go over there and pray." He took with him Peter and the two sons of Zebedee. Grief and anguish came over him, and he said to them, "The sorrow in my heart is so great that it almost crushes me. Stay here and keep watch with me."

He went a little farther on, threw himself face downward on the ground, and prayed, "My Father, if it is possible, take this cup of suffering from me! Yet not what I want, but what you want."

Then he returned to the three disciples and found them asleep; and he said to Peter, "How is it that you three were not able to keep watch with me for even one hour? Keep watch and pray that you will not fall into temptation. The spirit is willing, but the flesh is weak."

Once more Jesus went away and prayed, "My Father, if this cup of suffering cannot be taken away unless I drink it, your will be done." He returned once more and found the disciples asleep; they could not keep their eyes open.

Again Jesus left them, went away and prayed the third time, saying the same words. Then he returned to the disciples and said, "Are you still sleeping and resting? Look! The hour has come for the Son of Man to be handed over to the power of sinful men. Get up, let us go. Look, here is the man who is betraying me!"

Jesus was still speaking when Judas, one of the twelve disciples, arrived. With him was a large crowd armed with swords and clubs and sent by the chief priests and the elders. The traitor had given the crowd a signal: "The man I kiss is the one you want. Arrest him!"

Judas went straight to Jesus and said, "Peace be with you, Teacher," and kissed him.

Jesus answered, "Be quick about it, friend!"

Then they came up, arrested Jesus, and held him tight. One of those who were with Jesus drew his sword and struck at the High Priest's slave, cutting off his ear. "Put your sword back in its place," Jesus said to him. "All who take the sword will die by the sword. Don't you know that I could call on my Father for help, and at once he would send me more than twelve armies of angels? But in that case, how could the Scriptures come true which say that this is what must happen?"

Then Jesus spoke to the crowd, "Did you have to come with swords and clubs to capture me, as though I were an outlaw? Every day I sat down and taught in the Temple, and you did not arrest me. But all this has happened in order to make come true what the prophets wrote in the Scriptures."

Then all the disciples left him and ran away—*Matthew 26: 36-56*

"The sorrow almost crushes me"

The only one of the Twelve who was alert that night was Judas, and he was bent on Jesus' destruction. It was too bad, for if ever Jesus needed friends, it was during those last few hours before his arrest.

After the supper, they went to a garden outside the city. Judas, of course, had left during the supper to make arrangements for Christ's arrest. The garden would be an ideal place for the ambush: he had often gone there before, and they could seize him without the populace being aware of it. The authorities were afraid to make an arrest in public; his followers might provoke a riot.

Jesus and his friends were quiet as they entered the garden. He was silent and withdrawn, and they felt a sense of foreboding. The dinner, the wine, and their nameless fears made them tired and sleepy. They wouldn't be of much help to him tonight.

As the crisis drew near, Jesus experienced an overpowering feeling of sorrow, fear, and loneliness. He realized that terrible things were about to happen to him . . . and he wanted out. He felt the on-rush of terror and dread, and he wanted to run away from the whole thing.

There have always been people who believed that Jesus was the Son of God but who could not quite convince themselves that he was truly human like you and me. Without putting it into words, they have thought of him as God playing a part, making believe he was human. But that's not the way it was. He experienced to the full all the frailties (except sin) that are part of the human condition. His sorrow, his fear, his loneliness were all too real. They almost defeated him.

In this crisis, as he has done before, he tries to pray. But his Father seems remote, aloof, far away. In desperation he asks to be spared the ordeal that's rushing upon him, but even as the words escape his lips he rejects them. A titanic struggle is being waged within his soul. "My Father, if it is possible, take this cup of suffering from me! Yet not what I want, but what you want." He knows in his heart of hearts that his ordeal will end in triumph, and that it is of tremendous importance to others.

He brings his burden not only to God but also to his friends, so they can share it with him. Although he goes off by himself, he leads Peter, James and John to a spot close by. These are the three who saw his glory on the mount of Transfiguration. Now they will see him at his lowest point, beaten, and crushed by the terror that drains the very blood from his pores. He wants them to hear his prayer, to know how he feels, to share his loneliness and fear. He's saying, "Look, I can't take this thing by myself. Please help me. I need you."

At this desperate moment he prays and then comes over to find them asleep. He wakes them up and asks them to share his prayer. Guilt and shame make them promise to stand by him, but weariness lulls them to sleep again, leaving him terribly alone. If he had asked them to draw swords and fight, they would probably have sprung to his aid. But this time he didn't want them to *do* anything; he just wanted them to *be* there with him in his hour of need, and they failed him. The one time that God needed us humans, we let him down.

We all have the experience, too many times, of being let down by people. Friends are rarely as dependable as we want them to be. Sometimes we cope with this by trying to cut ourselves off from all dependence on others, by pursuing the unattainable goal of self-sufficiency. Or by amassing wealth and power over others, we try to guarantee that help will never be lacking, because we've bought it with money or influence. These are ways we try to escape from the human condition, which decrees that people will always need people, no matter how shaky or unsatisfactory the arrangement. When God became one of us in Jesus Christ, he went all the way, even to depending on weak, sinful people who deserted him in his hour of greatest need. This is how he tells us that if we want to become real people, we must count on others, even at the risk of betrayal.

Speaking of betrayals . . . here comes Judas with his motley band of Temple guards and security police. Judas and Jesus meet for the last time in the murky groves of Gethsemane, whose shadows mirror the darkness in the traitor's heart. Christ is face to face with his most spectacular failure. It may seem strange to say it, but you could make out a good case for describing Jesus as an underachiever. After all, his main work was with people. And here, a few hours before his death, what has he accomplished? A trusted friend betrays him, and his inner circle of followers run from the garden in panic. Tomorrow the crowd, which has never understood him, will cry for his blood, and his enemies' triumph will be complete. It's no exaggeration to say that few people have had as little to show for their lives, at the moment of death, as did Jesus of Nazareth. The ultimate humiliation, the kiss of Judas, said it all.

Things to do

1. Have you ever had to cope with fear in order to do something important? How did you handle it? Did you ever pray in such a situation? Was your prayer answered?
2. Do you think Jesus' friends were less dependable than most?
3. Have you ever been let down by people you depended on? Or did you ever disappoint someone who needed your help?
4. Would we do better if we didn't need people or depend on them?
5. Is it accurate to describe Jesus as a failure?

The Judgment of Pilate

Early in the morning all the chief priests and the elders made their plans against Jesus to put him to death. They put him in chains, led him off, and handed him over to Pilate, the Roman governor.

They began to accuse him: "We caught this man misleading our people, telling them not to pay taxes to the Emperor and claiming that he himself is the Messiah, a king."

Pilate went back into the palace and called Jesus. "Are you the king of the Jews?" he asked him.

Jesus answered, "Does this question come from you or have others told you about me?"

Pilate replied, "Do you think I am a Jew? It was your own people and the chief priests who handed you over to me. What have you done?"

Jesus said, "My kingdom does not belong to this world; if my kingdom belonged to this world, my followers would fight to keep me from being handed over to the Jewish authorities. No, my kingdom does not belong here!"

So Pilate asked him, "Are you a king, then?"

Jesus answered, "You say that I am a king. I was born and came into the world for this one purpose, to speak about the truth. Whoever belongs to the truth listens to me."

"And what is truth?" Pilate asked.

Pilate called together the chief priests, the leaders, and the people, and said to them, "You brought this man to me and said that he was misleading the people. Now, I have examined him here in your presence, and I have not found him guilty of any of the crimes you accuse him of. Nor did Herod find him guilty, for he sent him back to us. There is nothing this man has done to deserve death. So I will have him whipped and let him go."

Then Pilate took Jesus and had him whipped. The soldiers made a crown out of thorny branches and put it on his head; then they put a purple robe on him and came to him and said, "Long live the King of the Jews!" And they went up and slapped him.

Pilate went back out once more and said to the crowd, "Look, I will bring him out here to you to let you see that I cannot find any reason to condemn him." So Jesus came out, wearing the crown of thorns and the purple robe. Pilate said to them, "Look! Here is the man!"

When the chief priests and the temple guards saw him, they shouted, "Crucify him! Crucify him!"

Pilate said to them, "You take him, then, and crucify him. I find no reason to condemn him."

The crowd answered back, "We have a law that says he ought to die, because he claimed to be the Son of God."

When Pilate heard this, he was even more afraid. He went back into the palace and asked Jesus, "Where do you come from?"

But Jesus did not answer. Pilate said to him, "You will not speak to me? Remember, I have the authority to set you free and also to have you crucified."

Jesus answered, "You have authority over me only because it was given to you by God. So the man who handed me over to you is guilty of a worse sin."

When Pilate heard this, he tried to find a way to set Jesus free. But the crowd shouted back, "If you set him free, that means you are not the Emperor's friend! Anyone who claims to be a king is a rebel against the Emperor!"

When Pilate saw that it was no use to go on, but that a riot might break out, he took some water, washed his hands in front of the crowd, and said, "I am not responsible for the death of this man! This is your doing!"

Then Pilate handed Jesus over to them to be crucified.— *Matthew 27:1-2; Luke 23:2; John 18:33-38; Luke 23:13-16; John 19:1-12; Matthew 27:24; John 19:16*

"And what is truth?"

In the final scene of the movie *Judgment at Nuremberg,* Spencer Tracy confronts Burt Lancaster in the latter's prison cell. Tracy, an American jurist, has sentenced Lancaster, a convicted Nazi war criminal. As a civil judge, Lancaster had bowed to pressure from Hitler and had knowingly condemned innocent defendants, who were then sent to the concentration camps. In the film, Lancaster acknowledges his guilt and the justice of his sentence, but in a final private meeting he pleads with Tracy not to judge him too harshly in his mind: "I want you to know . . . you must understand . . . I never thought it would come to this [the concentration camps]." Tracy looks long and hard at him, and the movie audience expects a word of pardon, or at least of understanding, a recognition that he did not foresee the horror of the camps. Instead, he says: "It came to this the first time you condemned an innocent man."

The cell door clangs shut, Tracy leaves, and the film ends.

Pontius Pilate never thought it would come to crucifixion. True, the case of the Priests vs. Jesus would not have come before him if the plaintiffs were not seeking the death penalty. Under the terms of the occupation of Judea, the death sentence was reserved to the Roman governor. But he was confident he could settle the case without taking any extreme measures. Throughout the hours of that Friday morning, he twisted and turned and tried every gambit he knew, to save the life of this apparently harmless man. But he lost the fight, and Jesus forfeited his life, almost at the very start of the proceedings.

After hearing the charges of sedition, he examines the defendant, is convinced of his innocence, and so informs his accusers: "I cannot find any reason to condemn him." And that should have been the end of it, right there. His next words should have been, "Therefore I will let him go." Instead, he makes a fatal error. He tries to compromise, to come up with something for everybody. The governor had the power to ram an acquittal down their throats, but politics and public relations made it advisable for him to get along with the Temple authorities and avoid friction as much as possible. That was Roman policy in occupied territories. If he just did the right thing and let Jesus go free, the religious leaders would lose face.

So, to sweeten the pill of an adverse judgment, he decrees: "I will have him whipped and let him go."

Punish him for what? For being innocent? For being falsely accused? For getting caught in the middle of a power struggle between corrupt and powerful men? Pilate thought he could have it both ways. He forgot that justice and compromise almost never go together.

It is fascinating and disturbing to trace the steps of that morning's encounter between Jesus and Pilate. At first the governor is haughty and detached, intent on dispensing impersonal justice. But as the drama progresses, he is struck by the quiet dignity and strength of the prisoner. It unsettles him, makes him less sure of himself. "You will not speak to me? Remember, I have the authority to set you free and also to have you crucified." During the course of the interrogations there is a subtle reversal of roles, so that Jesus sounds like the judge and Pilate like the accused: "You have authority only because it was given to you by God. So the man who handed me over to you is guilty of a worse sin."

The governor, thrown off balance by this disquieting man, realizes at one point that he is in danger of being personally touched by him. We have witnessed this phenomenon before. Remember Zacchaeus? The Samaritan woman? Like them, Pilate came under Jesus' spell and almost found his inner, rock-bottom self. Just in time, he stepped back and put on one of the masks we all save for those occasions when we want to avoid seeing ourselves for what we really are. This was the mask of the sophisticated skeptic, the cultivated Roman who spurned religion as superstition. "Do you think I am a Jew? . . . And what is truth?"

Still he tries to avoid a total sellout. He wants the impossible: to be fair, but not *too* fair. He wants to dispense justice, but not *too* much. He wants to tell the truth, but not at the expense of important people's feelings. He wants to respect religion, but not get involved in it. Why can't the priests be more reasonable? Why won't Jesus bend a little and help him? Damn these single-minded, fanatical Jews! No wonder they're down and Rome is up! They don't know the First Rule for Getting Ahead! "To get along, you go along."

He's holding out, playing for time, but the priests know he's hooked, and all they have to do is reel him in. At last they play their trump card: "If you release this man, you are no friend of Caesar."

That does it. When the chips are down, you have to stick up for what's important. If he doesn't commit judicial murder and execute

Jesus, these vengeful men will see to it that Caesar, back in Rome, gets a bad report on him. Think what that would mean: No more governor's palace, with free limousine service and padded expense account. No more swimming pool. Goodbye stereo system and dancing girls. Etc., etc., etc. Okay, guys, you win. Take him away. Just give me some water, so I can wash his blood off my hands. Don't blame me: it's his own fault. A man has to protect his own. I mean, survival is what it's all about, right? I didn't want to hurt anybody, just do right by my family. A lot of people depend on me, and I owe them something. But I never thought it would come to this.

Things to do

1. Why did the Jewish leaders have to bring Jesus before Pilate?
2. What was the governor's first tactical error in his attempt to save Jesus?
3. Why was Pilate so anxious to compromise?
4. Which argument by Jesus' enemies assured his conviction? What was the weakness in Pilate that made that argument decisive?
5. Does this sort of thing go on today? Where? Are the same causes at work?
6. What were the qualities of Jesus, besides his evident innocence, that troubled Pilate?
7. Would Pilate have been better off if he had never met Jesus? Were there other people in Jesus' life who turned out worse for having met him? Who? How do you explain this?

The Cross

So they took Jesus away, scourged him and crowned him with thorns, dragged him outside the city and crucified him.

From Gethsemane to Calvary, the physical sufferings he undergoes are so barbaric that we shrink in horror from contemplating them. But the torments he endures are not only of the body but also of the mind, the spirit, the feelings, the emotions.

He experiences distress and fear and the overpowering desire to run away from it all. Betrayed and abandoned by his friends, he knows what it is to be alone. Promises made to him are broken. He is falsely accused, interrogated and judged by hypocrites. He is blindfolded, made the butt of jokes, and brutally struck. They drag him through the streets, dress him up like a king, and treat him like a fool.

As he hangs on the cross in excruciating pain, he is despised, gloated over, and mocked. Nearly all his friends have run away. A tremendous sense of loneliness and depression comes over him, the feeling of being totally alone and utterly helpless. He feels that even his Father has abandoned him. In this extremity of bodily and mental anguish, he cries out, "My God, my God, why did you abandon me?" He receives no answer, no relief, and dies alone.

Think of the evil in your own life. Consider not only your personal sins but also all the sorrows, difficulties, and disorientations that afflict your body and mind. Omit nothing that is confusing, lonely, and painful. Include even the transition from this phase of your life to the next phase—the transition called death. And realize that *you no longer suffer these alone*. Christ has taken on everything in your life that brings you guilt, pain, confusion, loneliness, and fear. From now on you two share it together.

The theologian can identify the evil in your life in a minute but can't explain it in a lifetime.

The theologian can tell you that God can draw good from the evil in your life. This is fine as you sit there comfortably and listen. This is not fine when you begin to hurt.

When you hurt, theoretical explanations don't offer much comfort.

When you hurt—whether in your body, or in your feelings, in the midst of utter boredom or of such spiritual confusion that you don't even know if you believe or trust in God—perhaps all you can do at a time like that is cry "Help!" and ask Christ on the cross to take you by the hand.

Resurrection: Meeting with Disciples

It was late that Sunday evening, and the disciples were gathered together behind locked doors, because they were afraid of the Jewish authorities. Then Jesus came and stood among them. "Peace be with you," he said.

They were terrified, thinking that they were seeing a ghost. But he said to them, "Why are you alarmed? Why are these doubts coming up in your minds? Look at my hands and my feet, and see that it is I myself. Feel me, and you will know, for a ghost doesn't have flesh and bones, as you can see I have."

He said this and showed them his hands and his feet. They still could not believe, they were so full of joy and wonder; so he asked them, "Do you have anything here to eat?" They gave him a piece of cooked fish, which he took and ate in their presence.

Then he said to them, "These are the very things I told you about while I was still with you; everything written about me in the Law of Moses, the writing of the prophets, and the Psalms had to come true."

Then he opened their minds to understand the Scriptures . . . Jesus said to them again, "Peace be with you. As the Father sent me, so I send you." Then he breathed on them and said, "Receive the Holy Spirit. If you forgive people's sins, they are forgiven; if you do not forgive them, they are not forgiven."

One of the twelve disciples, Thomas (called the Twin), was not with them when Jesus came. So the other disciples told him, "We have seen the Lord!"

Thomas said to them, "Unless I see the scars of the nails in his hands and put my finger on those scars and my hand in his side, I will not believe."

A week later the disciples were together again indoors, and Thomas was with them. The doors were locked, but Jesus came and stood among them and said, "Peace be with you." Then he said to Thomas, "Put your finger here, and look at my hands; then reach out your hand and put it in my side. Stop your doubting, and believe!"

Thomas answered him, "My Lord and my God!"

Jesus said to him, "Do you believe because you see me? How happy are those who believe without seeing me!" —*John 20:19; Luke 24:37-45; John 20:21-29*

"It is I myself"

An old saying has it that it's never so dark as just before the dawn. This was certainly true for Jesus' followers on the first Easter Sunday.

This past week they'd had enough shocks to last them a lifetime. A week ago they had accompanied him on a triumphal march into Jerusalem to celebrate the feast of national liberation, the Passover. The waving palm branches and the enthusiastic shouts of the crowd created in them the illusion that they were in the front ranks of a popular movement destined to sweep all before it. They thought a revolution was in the offing and that they'd be the key people in the New Order, with Jesus at their head. How long ago that seemed now! The arrest of their leader on Thursday, his trial before Pilate on Friday and his swift and horrible execution seemed like a nightmare from which they couldn't awaken. All their hopes and ambitions lay in ruins, and they'd lost even the will to put the shattered pieces of their lives together again.

The scene we've quoted takes place in the evening. The disciples are huddled together in fear and grief. The authorities have done away with Jesus, and it might well be his friends' turn next. Terror has locked and bolted the doors of the supper room, but despair has locked their minds and hearts. Disillusionment has robbed them of their dreams. They're without hope, wallowing in self-pity, tortured by remorse, paralyzed by fear.

And it's at this moment of impenetrable gloom that the Light bursts upon them. Even though the doors are shut, Jesus comes and stands before them. Shalom, he says: "Peace."

The disciples panic. They've seen him dead and buried, so this must be a ghost. After all that's happened, this is just too much, and they're beside themselves with fright.

But he talks to them, gently, calmly, quieting their fear. "What are you afraid of? This isn't a disembodied spirit. It's really me. Look, I'm eating this fish; ghosts don't eat. Here, touch me. Don't be afraid." Gradually their fright and disbelief subside, and the peace he has wished them fills their hearts with a joy such as they've never known or dreamed of. Now calm mingles with their exhilaration, and he explains to them that he had to suffer and die, that he has risen from the dead, that his triumph is complete. They're together once more, and nothing can ever separate them again.

Remember, these are the same disciples who had abandoned him just a few days before. These are the friends who had sworn at the Last Supper that they'd stand by him, and then had run away.

"Peace," Christ says again. And this "Peace" is more than a greeting. It has a fullness of meaning, and part of that meaning is forgiveness of their failure.

Christ then gives them the awesome power to forgive sins. It's the right moment to confer this gift. Forgiveness is for *sinners,* and so it's to sinners that he gives the power to forgive. In effect, he's saying to them: "When others come to you with their sins and their faults, remember that you too have fallen on your face. Keep that in mind, and help them out, as I have helped you."

It's a medically-proven fact that some bones, after being broken and set, mend and become stronger than before. Relationships are subject to the same paradox. You'd think that friends who never disagreed would be closer than those who have broken up and come together again, but it isn't necessarily so. Lovers are rarely so close as when they've just kissed and made up after a quarrel. It was that way between Jesus and his followers, and it's that way between God and us. There's something special between the shepherd and the lost sheep, and it wouldn't be there if the sheep had never strayed from the flock. We're not saying that people should stray or sin. We're just paraphrasing Jesus himself, who said that there would be more joy in heaven over one repentant sinner than over ninety-nine who had nothing to repent. Don't try to figure it out. The heart has reasons that the mind can never understand.

* * * *

Thomas wasn't there for all of this. How fortunate for us! Whatever kept him away that first Easter Sunday evening, it was a good break for those of us who need a little extra help from our friends to believe the Good News.

Why didn't Thomas believe the others when they told him they had seen the Lord? Well, he had been burned once already. He had staked everything on Jesus, and had seen his hopes go down the drain on Good Friday. That kind of disillusionment he didn't need . . . not again. Thomas fell into the classic trap that most of us fall into at one time or another. He tried to insulate himself against disappointment by swearing off faith and trust. Fortunately, he didn't keep his pledge, or he would have shriveled up as a human being.

Jesus went an extra mile to save Thomas from his self-defeating, corrosive doubt. And in doing so, he spoke an encouraging word for all of us who, like Thomas, find it hard to believe and who would rather see for ourselves.

"Do you believe because you see me? How happy are those who believe without seeing me!"

We're tempted to envy the disciples, to wish that we could meet the risen Christ face to face as they did. We see that encounter as something very special. But Jesus tells us that *we* are the ones who are special, for we believe without seeing and thus accept from his hand the gift of faith. Nothing turned Jesus on more than people's faith in him. In this he was like most of us. And he hasn't changed a bit.

Things to do

1. Have you ever heard news that was too good to be believed?
2. Have you ever had the experience of quarreling with someone and then making up? Were you as close after the reconciliation?
3. Do you think that weak, sinful people should be given the power to forgive sin?
4. Why was Thomas unwilling to accept the disciples' story of the resurrection? Was his attitude unreasonable? How does it compare with the reaction of the other disciples when the women told them of finding Jesus' tomb empty *(Luke 24:1-10)*?
5. How can it be said that we who have never seen Jesus in the flesh are more fortunate than those who did?

The Walk to Emmaus

On that same day two of Jesus' followers were going to a village named Emmaus, about seven miles from Jerusalem, and they were talking to each other about all the things that had happened. As they talked and discussed, Jesus himself drew near and walked along with them; they saw him, but somehow did not recognize him. Jesus said to them, "What are you talking about to each other, as you walk along?"

They stood still, with sad faces. One of them, named Cleopas, asked him, "Are you the only visitor in Jerusalem who doesn't know the things that have been happening there these last few days?"

"What things?" he asked.

"The things that happened to Jesus of Nazareth," they answered. "This man was a prophet and was considered by God and by all the people to be powerful in everything he said and did. Our chief priests and rulers handed him over to be sentenced to death, and he was crucified. And we had hoped that he would be the one who was going to set Israel free! Besides all that, this is now the third day since it happened. Some of the women of our group surprised us; they went at dawn to the tomb, but could not find his body. They came back saying that they had seen a vision of angels who told them that he is alive. Some of our group went to the tomb and found it exactly as the women had said, but they did not see him."

Then Jesus said to them, "How foolish you are, how slow you are to believe everything the prophets said! Was it not necessary for the Messiah to suffer these things and then to enter his glory?" And Jesus explained to them what was said about himself in all the Scriptures, beginning with the books of Moses and the writings of all the prophets.

As they came near the village to which they were going, Jesus acted as if he were going farther; but they held him back, saying, "Stay with us; the day is almost over and it is getting dark." So he went in to stay with them. He sat down to eat with them, took the bread, and said the blessing; then he broke the bread and gave it to them. Then their eyes were opened, and they recognized him, but he disappeared from their sight. They said to each other, "Wasn't it like a fire burning in us when he talked to us on the road and explained the Scriptures to us?"

They got up at once and went back to Jerusalem, where they found the eleven disciples gathered together with the others and saying, "The Lord is risen indeed! He has appeared to Simon!" Then they told their story of what had happened on the road and how they had recognised him at the breaking of bread.—*Luke 24:13-35*

"Stay with us"

It was on the afternoon of that first Easter Sunday that Cleopas and his friend met the risen Jesus. There are many mysterious things about this meeting, but the first is that they didn't recognize him. There are several other instances in the gospel accounts of the post-resurrection Jesus in which the same thing happens: people who had been close to him in life do not know him at first, but then perceive his identity in a flash of recognition.

In all of these scenes, one thing must be kept in mind. The disciples are experiencing a reality which no words, no language, can fully express. We're dealing here with a mystery—the mystery of Christ's resurrected body.

As usual, there are two sides to the mystery: his resurrected body is *real,* and it is *changed.* Or put it another way: It's really Jesus, but he's different. His body is radically transformed, but not destroyed. He can eat, but he needs no food. He can be touched, yet he is free of the bounds of time and space. Radiant in triumph, he is forever more a stranger to weariness and pain and loneliness. He who drank the cup of suffering to the dregs and laid down his life has banished sorrow and defeated death.

But he looked like just another friendly stranger that Sunday afternoon, when he joined the two grieving disciples on the way to Emmaus. He shows an interest in them and expresses concern at their sadness and dejection. To his gentle prodding, they respond by unburdening themselves of their sorrow. They tell him of the terrible things that have happened, the great things that might have been, the beautiful things that now can never be. It's a story of dashed expectations and of dreams laid waste. "We had hoped . . . ," But we hope no longer. It's finished, and so are we.

Up to this point Jesus has just been a good listener. When people are down the way Cleopas and his friend were, the best thing we can give them is a willing ear. If I'm scraping the bottom and you're my friend, I don't want words from you. Just be with me, and care.

Jesus did that, and more. He speaks words not of empty comfort, but of brilliant insight. Recalling the history of their people, the story of God's ways with men, he helps the travelers to see that a

suffering Messiah meant, not the end of their hopes, but the fulfill-
ment of God's saving plan.

As they come under his spell, their burden somehow becomes
lighter, and they begin to feel at peace with themselves. Before they
know it, they've arrived at their destination.

Then the stranger says good-bye and makes as though to con-
tinue his journey. But they're concerned: it's getting dark, the roads
are unsafe, he's been on foot a long time. So they offer him their
hospitality: "Stay with us." Such a small gesture of thoughtfulness
. . . and such a great reward! In "the breaking of the bread"—a
phrase that sounds very much like the Eucharist—they experience
the unforgettable moment of recognition: it's he. And just as quickly
it's over, and he's gone.

"Wasn't it like a fire burning in us when he talked to us on the
road and explained the Scriptures to us?" Yes, and they know the
flame will never die. He has vanished from their sight, but no matter;
he lives. He's with them, and nothing can ever take him away. So this
is how we meet the risen Christ, you and I . . . through a kind word,
by an unselfish invitation, in the Breaking of the Bread. He comes
unexpectedly, is not always recognized, is glad to be asked, but forces
himself on no one. To see him, I must be as alert to the needs of
others as to my own. He waits for me—in the guise of a needy
stranger or a suffering friend, and under the appearances of bread
and wine. Only the eyes of faith can pierce the veil, but one moment
of vision is worth a lifetime.

Finally, to recognize the risen Jesus is to catch a glimpse of the
person I'm destined to be. When Christ conquered death, he did it
for us all. The gift of eternal life is offered to those who will take it.
What will that life be like? We don't know.

> What no one ever saw or heard, what no one ever thought
> could happen, is the very thing God prepared for those
> who love him.—*1 Corinthians 2:9*

But we're given a sign—the resurrected body of Jesus. Like
him, we will suffer and die, but we will not be destroyed. We will be
changed, remarkably changed for the better:

> Now God's home is with mankind! He will live with them,
> and they shall be his people. God himself will be with

them, and he will be their God. He will wipe away all tears from their eyes. There will be no more death, no more grief or crying or pain. The old things have disappeared.

—Revelation 21:3,4

And all our heart-wishes will be fulfilled, beyond our wildest dreams. When Christ triumphed in his resurrection, he defeated everything (including death) that is painful, confusing, difficult, lonely. By his total victory over sin and death he gained everything (including resurrection) that the heart can wish for.

Okay, so Jesus triumphed. (Nice going, Jesus!) But what does that have to do with me?

Everything. His resurrection is the source of every triumph in your life. Because he rose, you can now attain everything (including resurrection) that your heart can wish for.

By yourself, you can never gain these things. Together with the risen Christ, you can. From now on you two strive together to attain your heart-wishes. You are no longer alone.

Things to do

1. What are some of the other incidents in the risen life of Jesus when people did not recognize him?
2. How might today's feminists interpret the disciples' unwillingness to believe the women's story?
3. What were some of the Scripture passages that Jesus probably explained on the road to Emmaus?
4. How is Jesus' risen existence different from the life he knew before death? Does it tell us anything about ourselves?
5. If the two men had not invited the stranger to supper, they would have missed a vision of the risen Christ. Is Jesus trying to tell us something? What?

EPILOGUE

The Holy Spirit

SENT FORTH BY THE SPIRIT

The Holy Spirit

When the day of Pentecost came, all the believers were gathered together in one place. Suddenly there was a noise from the sky which sounded like a strong wind blowing, and it filled the whole house where they were sitting. Then they saw what looked like tongues of fire which spread out and touched each person there. They were all filled with the Holy Spirit and began to talk in other languages, as the Spirit enabled them to speak.

There were Jews living in Jerusalem, religious men who had come from every country in the world. When they heard this noise, a large crowd gathered. They were all excited, because each one of them heard the believers talking in his own language. In amazement and wonder they exclaimed, "These people who are talking like this are Galileans! How is it, then, that all of us hear them speaking in our own native languages? Amazed and confused, they kept asking each other, "What does this mean?"

But the others made fun of the believers, saying, "These people are drunk!"

Then Peter stood up with the other eleven apostles and in a loud voice began to speak to the crowd: "Fellow Jews and all of you who live in Jerusalem, listen to me and let me tell you what this means. These people are not drunk, as you suppose; it is only nine o'clock in the morning.

"Listen to these words, fellow Israelites! Jesus of Nazareth was a man whose divine authority was clearly proven to you by all the miracles and wonders which God performed through him. You yourselves know this for it happened here among you. In accordance with his own plan God had already decided that Jesus would be handed over to you; and you killed him by letting sinful men crucify him. He has been raised to the right side of God, his Father, and has received from him the Holy Spirit, as he had promised. What you now see and hear is his gift that he has poured out on us.

"All the people of Israel, then, are to know for sure that this Jesus, whom you crucified, is the one that God has made Lord and Messiah!"

When the people heard this, they were deeply troubled and said to Peter and the other apostles, "What shall we do, brothers?"

Peter said to them, "Each one of you must turn away from

his sins and be baptized in the name of Jesus Christ, so that your sins will be forgiven; and you will receive God's gift, the Holy Spirit. For God's promise was made to you and your children, and to all who are far away—all whom the Lord our God calls to himself."

Peter made his appeal to them and with many other words he urged them, saying, "Save yourselves from the punishment coming on this wicked people!" Many of them believed his message and were baptized, and about three thousand people were added to the group that day.

These remained faithful to the teaching of the apostles, to the brotherhood, to the breaking of bread and to the prayers.—*Acts 2:1-8, 12-15, 22-23, 33, 36-42*

It's too early to be drunk

The risen Jesus didn't stay long with his followers—just long enough to confirm their faith in him and in themselves, for the great work that was about to begin. He had told them he must go, so that he might send the Holy Spirit to confirm them in their mission of carrying the Good News to the ends of the earth.

When the Spirit came upon them, the results were spectacular. People were deeply moved. An extraordinary change came over them, and they began to understand, much more deeply, all that Christ said and did. Where at an earlier date all was confusion and "in one ear and out the other," now there is a profound experience of the meaning. They themselves have come alive as people. There's a courage and a strength that was missing before. There's a peace that isn't their own. There's a capacity to grow. There's a meeting with God, and in the Holy Spirit there's a meeting with others. From now on they belong to God and to one another.

And there's a desire to share all this with other people.

Notice the symbol of fire—a very apt symbol indeed. With one match I can start a bonfire. Fire spreads—and so will this community of Christ's friends called Church. So will this influence of the Holy Spirit. Prompted by the Spirit, Christ's friends want to share him with others.

Of course, no matter how marvelously God works among people, he doesn't overpower them and force them to believe. The response of faith is free. Even on this great day, there were a few wise guys who weren't impressed. These cynics kept their skepticism intact, and successfully resisted any danger of religious experience by making fun of the whole scene: "These people are all smashed; they're nuts." Peter has an easy answer for that one: It's only nine o'clock in the morning, much too early for all these people to be drunk.

Then Peter gets serious, and is inspired to make the best speech of his life. This man who, a couple of months ago, caved in before the taunts of a servant girl and denied Christ, now stands before his people and calls them to repent and be converted. He tells them of God's plan, of Christ, of the gift of the Spirit. And the people are shaken. They're deeply moved, and not just because of Peter's words. While Peter's words are reaching their ears, the Spirit is reaching their hearts. (That's the way it always is. Words, without the grace of the Spirit, never converted anybody.)

"What should we do?" they ask. "Each of you must turn away from his sins and be baptized," he tells them.

The word *reform* has a very deep meaning. Part of its meaning is that you must be willing to open up, be willing to change, to take a chance, to adventure toward God, Baptism will be a sign of this willingness to take up a whole new kind of life, if that's what God wants.

Throughout this scene we have God meeting people through people. That's the story of the Church—the community of Christ's friends which now begins to spread. From the very beginning, people who have heard the Good News of Jesus' life, death, and resurrection and who have responded in joy and faith, have tended to come together to celebrate and live what they've come to believe.

So Pentecost isn't the end of the Jesus story, but the beginning. The coming of God among us, and the pouring out of his Spirit, was not a one-shot deal that happened a long time ago. It's a continual encounter that takes place not only in the individual human heart but within the community of those who, despite all their differences, are made one through their faith in Jesus Christ, and who remain faithful "to the teaching of the apostles, to the brotherhood, to the breaking of bread and to the prayers."

The fire is still spreading. Do you feel it?

Things to do

1. This whole scene is so spectacular and so far removed from our everyday experience that the question arises: What can it say to us about the life of the Church as we know and experience it?

2. Do some research on the Pentecostal or charismatic movement in the Church. Interview some member(s) of a charismatic prayer group about the faith encounters they've experienced. What is the significance of this fast-growing, worldwide movement?

3. In the Gospel accounts and the Acts of the Apostles, trace the story of Peter before and after the coming of the Spirit. Does he change much? How do you account for this?

4. What do we learn from this account about the meaning of the sacrament of Confirmation?

5. Many today, especially young people, say they believe in Jesus Christ but can't find him in the Church. What message does Pentecost have for them? How would you apply it to yourself?